D1367994

Deer in My Garden

NIAGARA FALLS PUBLIC LIBRARY
1425 MAIN ST
NIAGARA FALLS NY 14305

Deer in My Garden

Vol. 1: Perennials & Subshrubs

by Carolyn Singer

THE YUCKY FLOWER SERIES®

ABOUT THE AUTHOR

Carolyn Singer is an enthusiastic gardener whose designs have been published in "Home Landscaping California Region", by Roger Holmes and Lance Walheim (published by Creative Homeowner Press, 2001). Her work is also mentioned in Judith M. Taylor's "Tangible Memories, Californians and Their Gardens, 1800-1850" (published 2003).

Carolyn's perennial nursery, Foothill Cottage Gardens, and display gardens in Grass Valley, California were open to the public for 25 years. Her nursery was recognized nationally in publications (*Organic Gardening, Fine Gardening, Country Gardening,* and *Sunset*) and in "Taylor's Guide to Specialty Nurseries". Garden classes and tours were held every year. She has also taught at Sierra College.

In 1995 she contributed to the updated Time-Life "Complete Gardener: Perennials". She is a member of the Perennial Plant Asociation (PPA).

HGTV's Paul James, "Gardening By the Yard" filmed a segment on rock gardening with Carolyn at her Grass Valley, California garden in 2003.

She has published garden articles in *Fine Gardening, Garden Gate, Better Homes and Gardens Special Interest Publications,* and *Sierra Heritage* magazine. She also had a weekly garden column for several years in Nevada County, California.

A lifetime University of California Master Gardener, Carolyn has been involved with several garden and agricultural projects in her rural community.

She continues to consult, teach, lecture, write, and design gardens in northern California.

ACKNOWLEDGMENTS

Many students, nursery customers, garden visitors, and clients have contributed to this book. How many times have I heard the question: "When are you going to write a book?" Thank you for your patience, your enthusiastic support, and your passion for gardens and gardening.

My thanks to the gardeners who allowed me to test plants in their gardens, knowing that the plant might disappear if the deer found it to their liking. While I do not agree with the pessimists who boldly state that the deer eat everything, I do agree that deer tastes are not entirely predictable. I needed lots of gardens and gardeners to help me with this book. Thank you all.

I want to express my deepest appreciation to my son Sean McMillin for his support and book cover design. His children have brought me even closer to the gardening world as I see it through their eyes. My graphic designer, Katy Hight, deserves special recognition for her talent and enthusiasm. She has been a faithful customer in my nursery for many years.

The summer of 2005 was spent writing in Seattle. Special thanks to Trapper Robbins and Roxanne Everett for the use of their house.

A heartfelt thanks to my gardening friends Joan Ballenger in Ashland and Bob Scheulen in Seattle for all their suggestions, and for having the patience and commitment to read all that I had written. Your input was invaluable. Thanks also to Kim Wells, who pointed out the importance of my grandson Marcus' suggestion of yucky flowers, and thought I should move it to the beginning of my introduction.

Deer in My Garden
Vol. 1: Perennials & Subshrubs
by Carolyn Singer

Copyright © 2006 by Carolyn Singer
Printed in the United States of America

Garden Wisdom Press
www.gardenwisdom.com

Cover design: Sean McMillin
Interior design: Katy Hight
Photography: Carolyn Singer

All rights reserved

Singer, Carolyn.
    Deer in my garden. Vol. 1, Perennials & subshrubs /
by Carolyn Singer.
    p. cm. -- (The yucky flower series)
    Includes index.
    ISBN 0-9774251-0-X (print ed.)
    ISBN 0-9774251-1-8 (CD ed.)
    ISBN 0-9774251-3-4 (PDF ed.)

    1. Gardening--Handbooks, manuals, etc. 2. Deer.
3. Perennials--Diseases and pests--Handbooks, manuals, etc.
4. Shrubs--Diseases and pests--Handbooks, manuals, etc.
I. Title. II. Series.

SB450.96.S56 2006   635.9'26965
                     QBI06-600044

CONTENTS

INTRODUCTION

"Grandma, why don't you grow yucky flowers?" "Why would I do that, Marcus?" I asked, respectful of his three-year-old wisdom. "Well," he replied, "the deer wouldn't eat yucky flowers!"

In that precious moment he gave me the solution! I had shown him where the deer had eaten every single flower and bud from my white Japanese windflowers (*Anemone* x *hybrida*), leaving only the stalks and the leaves. He thought about it for the next 10 minutes, then asked me his simple question. For 25 years I had been planting hundreds of plants to discover what the deer would leave untouched. Why not just grow yucky flowers?

My garden is a haven for the deer. I have enjoyed their presence while I gardened on this site of an old homestead in the Sierra Nevada foothills in northern California. My Australian shepherd "Angel" stayed near me in the garden for 17 of those years. She preferred to be in the house with me at the end of our gardening day. In her youth she went through a screen door one night to chase the deer from the garden. After that, I remembered to keep the doors closed so I could spend money on plants, not screens! The deer appreciated that, and moved very quickly into the main garden as darkness fell. On summer evenings lit by the full moon, they had to wait longer for me to finish my garden puttering.

A row of evergreens (incense cedar, Douglas fir, and Ponderosa pine) frames the western edge of the garden. A sprawling ranch-style house defines the northern edge, and a gravel driveway rims the south and east.

A very large grassy area, brown from several years of drought, filled the frame when I moved in and began this project in 1977. With the return of good rains that winter, violets, *Iris spuria*, Japanese flowering quince, lilac, and hundreds of species daffodils bloomed, the only introduced plants that had survived years of drought and inattention. It had been 50 years or more since a serious gardener had lived here.

The site was inspiring. At the base of Sonntag Hill, a level area was on a knoll with full-sun exposure most of the day. To the east was an open view of the Sierras. I could do nothing, and the natural landscape would be perfect. But I am a gardener, and so began a project of redefinition and renewal. The introduction of many trees eventually gave welcome shade in the summer heat, and ornamental shrubs defined garden rooms. Perennials and subshrubs (those wonderful small shrubs) filled borders that grew larger each year.

I like to have wildlife in my garden. The California quail are frequent visitors by the dozens. Beyond my five acres, manzanita, pines, and other Sierra foothills natives harbor coyotes, raccoons, possums, fox, bobcats, black bear, an occasional cougar, and too many deer to count.

The deer are welcome. Last year a doe and her two spotted babies were frequent spring visitors in midday. She would graze on the grass and search for the few remaining asters in a nearby border. One fawn would stay close to her, and the other would run full speed around the garden paths. I watched from inside the house, appreciative of the safe zone my garden provided.

Sitting on a bench on a quiet evening, I could hear the sucking sounds of a fawn with its mother. What a gift!

I am learning, always. Two years ago, a young doe and her fawn spent most of the early summer in my bed of lily-of-the-valley. Of course they ate their bed! And so *Convallaria majalis*, which had been on my list of deer-resistant plants for years, was quietly removed.

One year I was writing an article about asters for Better Homes & Gardens Special Interest Publications (*Flower Garden*, May 1998). I encouraged my editor to promote the "deer-resistance" of this wonderful genus. I finished the article, emailed before the deadline, and went into the garden to renew my energy. The night before, the deer had stripped all the asters for the first time ever! I revised my approach to the article.

The deer have enjoyed my gardening (and writing?) efforts! I have often joked with my students, clients, and nursery customers that the more you spend, the more the deer will love your choice of plants.

For the past 10 years, I have been giving plants to gardeners in nearby deer areas to test for "deer-resistance". I have also shared notes with gardeners in other areas of California, in Oregon, Washington, British Columbia, and occasionally in the eastern United States. If there is a regional difference, this is supported by a recent article in *Fine Gardening* magazine (#104, August 2005). Some of the plants listed as deer-resistant in the midwest (*Aquilegia* and *Rosa rugosa*) are eaten by the deer in my California Sierra foothill garden.

I am a western gardener, having lived and gardened in the Sierra foothills (27 years), the San Francisco Bay area, Montana, and Colorado. When I was growing up, my family gardened in one of the best growing areas of California: Sonoma County, home to Luther Burbank. Great aunts, transplanted from England, inspired my early passion for flowers and earth. I have also spent a lot of time in the Pacific northwest, to observe the growing and blooming habits of perennials and other plants, to compare climates and microclimates, and to listen to deer stories.

For the past 25 years I have been teaching garden classes. My garden has provided a testing ground, and an example for the many students who have come to classes. The perennial nursery has been an extension of the garden. The deer-resistant section has been open to the deer and the customers.

Too many "deer-resistant" plant lists are compilations from other lists. I am including in this book a list of perennials and subshrubs that are often on these lists, but that have consistently been eaten by the deer (the plants, not the lists!) in the foothills. Gardeners need to share real gardening experiences and wisdom.

It is tempting to include plants that are only occasionally eaten. However, my experiences in the nursery and garden guide me to recommend only those perennials and subshrubs that the deer have *not* eaten, in all the geographical areas in which I have landscaped or shared observations with other gardeners.

This book is my list, based on more than 27 years of gardening in deer country. I hope my list of "yucky flowers" will work for other gardeners in deer country.

PLANNING AND PLANTING IN DEER COUNTRY

Each plant is detailed for its description, bloom, cultural requirements, seasonal interest, companion plants and landscape use, propagation, and maintenance.

Description, with height and spread, gives you the information you need for proper placement of each plant. Always plan for the eventual spread. A plant crowding, or crowded by, its neighbor may lose its value in the landscape.

Gardeners should be patient. If a plant is described as spreading, individual plants may be put closer together to fill in more quickly. If a plant is described as a good individual specimen, give each one room to show off. A perennial may be described as herbaceous (dying back to the root in winter) or evergreen.

Some species and cultivars of perennials or subshrubs within a genus (e.g. *Lavandula*) have common characteristics and are grouped together. Others (e.g. *Achillea*) are separated because they are distinctly different.

Cultural requirements will vary from region to region. USDA zones are helpful, with temperature range for winter. However, there is often a difference between references for the recommended zones for a particular plant.

A plant that is not recommended for cold winter areas may, in fact, grow there. Experienced gardeners in your area may be able to provide more specific regional information for your zone, microclimates (elevation, exposure, and weather) and plant requirements. Also check with nearby botanical gardens. Several sources, including gardeners, were used to establish the zone recommendations in this book.

The American Horticultural Society has also published a "Plant Heat-Zone Map" which is very helpful for summer "hardiness".

Soil pH has not been addressed for each plant. Know your area. Soils 6.5 to 7.5 are in a good range to release other essential nutrients, such as phosphorus. If you garden in acidic soils with a pH below 6.5, add oyster shell (5 pounds per 100 square feet) to raise the pH when you prepare the soil. Additional applications every other year at the same rate are beneficial. Gardeners with alkaline soils may use amendments that are acidic, and will not need to use oyster shell.

Whether your garden has clay or sandy soils, the plants detailed in this book will do better when organic compost has been added. Compost aerates the soil and adds nutrients. Explore the products that are available in your region, and choose an amendment that is composted. Wood-based products frequently lack nutrients and may tie up nitrogen when added to your soil. Read the label! A good product may contain animal manure or seaweed, or both.

A general rule for adding amendments is one-third compost to two-thirds native soil. A "lean" soil is a one to four ratio, and a "rich" soil is usually one-half compost and one-half native soil. Soils in some areas need more compost, while a few regions have naturally very fertile soils, and may need less.

The addition of an organic phosphorus will strengthen roots, increase flowering, and ensure greater drought-tolerance. Soft rock phosphate is an excellent source of phosphorus. A recommended application rate for those soils low in phosphorus is 15 to 20 pounds per hundred square feet. All plants in all soils will benefit from the addition of soft rock phosphate. Add a generous handful of the phosphorus with each plant. This organic form will not burn roots. Because it is not water-soluble, it must be incorporated into the soil, along with oyster shell in acid soils, when you prepare the soil for planting.

Mulches are very important to protect shallow roots, reduce moisture loss, and to prevent soil compaction from heavy rains or hail. In new plantings, cover the soil around your plant with two inches of compost, or a mix of decomposed straw and leaves. When you are renewing the mulch each year, cover the crown of a mature perennial with only a half-inch of compost, and keep the mulch around the plant at least 3 inches deep. Wood chips may be used as a "finish", but should not be your primary mulch. Some perennials, such as *Lavandula*, should have a gravel or gritty mulch to protect the lower foliage from moisture.

Irrigation requirements vary according to soils, climate, microclimate, season, and plant need. Evapotranspiration refers to the "loss" of moisture from the soil due to environmental factors. Sun, wind, climate, microclimate, weather, and even elevation all influence available moisture.

In my garden, the clay loam holds moisture. In the heat of the summer, 1½ inches of water will replace the available moisture in the top 12 inches of clay loam. The rock garden and dry gardens receive this amount every 3 weeks, while most of the borders are watered each week.

Planted in fall, which is the best season for landscaping in many areas, new perennials (even those that are "drought-tolerant") will need irrigation every 5 to 7 days the following spring and summer. Sun and wind will both effect loss of available moisture. Mulch your plantings!

In the first few months after planting, check the plant closely. If soil has settled and surface roots are exposed, renew the mulch. This is important in all seasons.

As plants mature, their roots are deeper. Irrigation may not be required as often, but the amount of irrigation is important. In clay loam, 1½ inches of water will replace the available moisture in the top 12 inches of soil. In the heat of summer, a plant needing regular irrigation will need to be watered every 7 to 10 days. Drought-tolerant plants may be watered every 2 to 3 weeks, or less.

Gardeners with sandy loam may irrigate more frequently, with 1 inch of water replacing the available moisture. This is why, in the Pacific Northwest where rains may be more frequent in the summer, no supplemental irrigation is required for drought-tolerant perennials and subshrubs. Cloudy days also lessen the drying impact of the sun.

Seasonal interest is why we garden. A plant that has several seasons of interest, or a long season of bloom, has strong value for the landscape. However, a perennial with a very dynamic but short period of bloom may be as coveted. Each year, I wait with great anticipation for the opening of the Oriental poppies in May and will not take trips away from my garden during those two weeks.

Bloom description helps with color choices, but remember that flowering may be a fleeting reward. Leaf color and form are most often dominant in the border for a longer period than the flowers. Green and gray are colors too, and so many different shades!

Place cut flowers in warm water. Dry flowers in shade. Save seedpods for seeds or everlastings from mature plants, not from young plants (1 to 2 years old) that should put their energy into growing. Everlastings are dried plant material: flowers, buds, seedheads, or foliage.

The time of bloom and even the length of bloom will depend on many factors. Your general geographical region, and within that, your particular microclimates are the first parameters to consider. A design for southwestern areas or eastern areas of the United States will not work for the foothills of the Sierra Nevada mountain range. Despite the photos, these perennials will not be in bloom at the same time. Work within what is known for your area, then consider your particular microclimates.

In cool climates, where summer temperatures are below 85°F, bloom length of most of perennials will be longer. However, within a cool climate, a very warm exposure (for example, reflected heat from a sidewalk or building) creates a microclimate that will result in an earlier timing of bloom, and a shortening of the length of time that the perennial continues to bloom.

Weather in any given year will also determine when and how long perennials bloom. Hotter summer temperatures, above 85°F, will shorten bloom. A cold, wet spring may delay bloom. One summer we planned a border for a spring wedding the following year. Using our records of bloom dates, mature perennials were moved in fall. The weather the following spring delayed bloom, which was perfect three weeks after the event!

Companion plants and landscape use for each perennial or subshrub are recommended, but the gardener should be experimental. As long as plants with similar cultural requirements (soil, sunlight exposure, and irrigation) are grouped together, many combinations may be pleasing.

Border refers to any planted area near a lawn, path, driveway, or building. It may include herbaceous perennials (those that are dormant in winter), subshrubs (small woody shrubs) that are deciduous or evergreen (or evergray), and larger trees and ornamental shrubs.

Color echoes, the repetition of like colors, may be subtle or strong. Flower petals or centers, sepals, seedheads, and leaves each may play a part in this artistic dynamic. Complementary colors may also be understated or bold. Buy a color wheel at an art supply store, and play with contrasting complementary colors. The effects of color echoes or complementary colors in the border can be stunning.

When two or more plants are recommended as companions, irrigation must address the plant with the higher needs. For example, an area with a *Caryopteris* needing irrigation once every 2 to 3 weeks in the heat of summer, next to a *Lavandula,* which needs little or no water, would be irrigated according to the needs of the *Caryopteris*. Plants chosen as companions, such as the *Lavandula* in this case, are compatible with the higher irrigation schedule.

Many bulbs may be planted near drought-tolerant or low-irrigation perennials. Fading bulb foliage from early-flowering bulbs (*Crocus, Puschkinia, Scilla, Galanthus*) may even be covered as herbaceous plants grow in the spring.

Consider the mature spread of each plant. If one plant spreads to 2 feet and another to 3 feet, add these mature spreads together and divide by two. The two plants would need to be planted 2½ feet apart, crown center to crown center. Do not overcrowd your plantings. The beauty of most perennials is in their leaf color and plant form. Flower color is often fleeting.

Create a quiet shady area for summer; this will be the best place to be in your garden on a hot day. A spring focal area might highlight several plants, visible from both inside the house and in the garden, near a bench. My entry garden pairs late bloomers near shrubs and small trees with good fall color. And it also includes some evergreens for winter interest.

Propagation methods vary. Recommended will be those methods that are easiest. Divisions and vegetative propagation (cuttings taken from terminal growth when flowering buds are not forming) may be the best method to increase your numbers of plants quickly. When rooted cuttings have been potted up, they often grow quickly, supplying more vegetative cuttings.

Take cuttings early in the morning, before sun hits the parent plant. Keep them shaded (no direct sunlight) and misted until roots have formed, which usually takes about 4 to 6 weeks.

Seeds are often difficult to germinate. This method of propagation is recommended for a perennial only if the seeds germinate easily or the plant self-sows. Some plants drop the seed, which germinates when conditions are agreeable. Mulch these plants before the seed is dispersed. Fall leaves often cover the seed, preventing germination, and should be removed. The seeds of plants that self-sow do not need to be covered. They need light to germinate.

Seed should be stored where it is cool and dry.

Young seedlings need moisture. A prolonged dry spell in winter may make irrigation necessary.

Maintenance differs for each plant and each gardener. If it offends you, cut it back!

Plan your garden so that you can reach plants that need attention during the spring or summer.

Some perennials need deadheading, the removal of faded flowers. This will often extend the blooming period. For example, a *Gaillardia* that is not deadheaded will put all its energy into developing seed, and flowering will decrease markedly.

Mulches for heat-loving or drought-tolerant perennials and subshrubs such as *Lavandula* or *Perovskia,* may be gravel or rocks.

Many perennials and subshrubs need no maintenance except during the dormant season. Woody subshrubs such as *Lavandula* or *Caryopteris clandonensis* need late-winter pruning, and may also be pruned right after bloom.

Evergreen subshrubs such as rosemary or sage may be shaped with light pruning. If you grow rosemary in a climate where the temperature goes below 15°F in winter, do not prune late in the summer or fall, except for light harvest of the herbs for soup at any time of the year. Pruning stimulates new, tender growth that may die back in winter.

When you are cutting back an herbaceous plant in any season, do not leave stems. "Cut back to the crown" means exactly that: all stems are cut to where they originate. Plants are much more attractive when new growth is not unfolding through dead stems! For example, Shasta daisies cut back to the crown after bloom will form new leaves that are very pleasing in the late summer and fall garden.

Achillea millefolium

ACHILLEA

Achillea filipendulina
(fern-leaf yarrow)

DESCRIPTION

Fern-leaf yarrow foliage is very interesting, with 10-inch long gray-green leaves, divided into segments, giving the appearance of fern fronds. In poor, unimproved soil, the plant grows to about 2 to 3 feet in height, with flower stalks to 3 to 4 feet. In compost-enriched growing beds, the gardener should expect a large plant! Roots are strong and deep when the plant is mature, enabling fern-leaf yarrow to survive hot dry summers without irrigation.

CULTURAL REQUIREMENTS

Zones 3–10. Full sun to very light shade. Thriving even with neglect, *Achillea filipendulina* is one of the best of the drought-tolerant perennials. In the wild garden, or "rugged zone", fern-leaf yarrow will grow in poor, rocky, clay or sandy soil. In the irrigated border where compost has been added, do not over-water. In sandy soils, irrigation every week may be tolerated, but in clay soils, this would be over-irrigation. Limit irrigation in heavier clay soils to once every 2 to 3 weeks. This perennial needs no irrigation in my hot summer climate. Yellow leaves are most often a sign of overwatering.

BLOOM

Named cultivars have different sizes of bloom. In my garden, the first blooms of 'Gold Plate' are 3 to 4 inches across, and side blooms are somewhat smaller. Plants coming up in the good soil in my vegetable garden were so happy, the largest blooms were 5 inches in diameter! The gold flowers are striking in the summer garden, strongest in the early summer.

For everlastings, cut a few stalks at the height of the color, before they begin to fade. The smaller heads on side shoots are nice for smaller flower arrangements. With strong stalks, this perennial does not need staking unless you overhead water or garden in an area of heavy summer downpours.

SEASONAL INTEREST

Summer is the best! But the attractive foliage is nice throughout the season, so plant a few where you will notice. Perhaps near the mailbox? In milder climates, the fern-leaf yarrow foliage is evergreen. Midwinter is the time to enjoy the dried flowers you picked in June or July.

COMPANION PLANTS & LANDSCAPE USES

Because this sturdy perennial is in my dry border, it is growing near *Romneya coulteri* (matilija poppy, fried-egg plant). What a duo! The strong gold of the yarrow is an echo of the golden center in the poppies. The white of the poppies seems to enrich the gold, adding a glow to my dry border. Another good companion is Russian sage (*Perovskia atriplicifolia*), which adds blue-violet, a complementary color.

A bulb that would be fun to add to a planting of fern-leaf yarrow is the drumstick allium (*Allium sphaerocephalum*). In the fall, plant bulbs in clusters of five to seven near the yarrow plants, but at least 1 foot from the edge of the yarrow crown. The strong stalks of the allium will come up through the new yarrow foliage in the spring, and in June the small purple *Allium* flowerheads will drift through the golden yarrow. As the burst of color fades on both flowers, the seedheads will still be an interesting combination.

PROPAGATION

Easy from seed, *Achillea filipendulina* self-sows even in the dry border. The seed must also blow in the wind, as new plants appear yards away from the stand of yarrow. Because this yarrow does not spread by runners, don't panic when you find a few volunteers here and there in the garden.

The seeds of yarrow are very fine. Sow them on top of the compost mulch and do not cover the seed. Irrigation or rains will nestle the seed down into the medium.

Older plants may also be divided, but do this task in the winter before the new spring growth starts. If weather delays division, and the yarrow is affected by spring warmth, the divisions may need to be cut back to avoid transplant shock.

MAINTENANCE

Deadheading isn't necessary, since the yarrow seedheads are so interesting. However, if the first flowering heads are removed as they fade, the remaining side shoots may have larger blooms.

Winter snows end the season, but until they do, the faded seedheads are attractive in the dry border. Cut the plant back to the crown in the middle of winter, well before new growth starts. This is a good time to mulch the yarrow plants with some compost to renew their vigor for next season's show.

Mulch will also help conserve moisture in the soil after spring rains stop. Use decomposing straw, a mulch that prevents the soil surface from drying out, and adds a food source for the earthworms. If you don't like its appearance, you can cover it with a layer of bark, chips or compost.

Achillea millefolium

(thousand-leafed yarrow, milfoil, common yarrow)

An aggressively spreading evergreen perennial when it is introduced into a garden, *Achillea millefolium* makes one of the best lawns for dry climates. Native to the Sierra Nevada mountains, this common yarrow should not be used in herbaceous flower borders or the small garden. It is recommended here only as a low-irrigation lawn or groundcover. And it is fire-retardent!

DESCRIPTION

Leaves are narrow with a ferny appearance, mid to dark-green. The plant spreads aggressively by stolons. Height of the leaves and the white flowers varies considerably, depending on soil fertility and irrigation.

CULTURAL REQUIREMENTS

Achillea millefolium

Zones 2–10. This evergreen wildflower will grow in the coldest regions of the western, southwestern, and northwestern United States.

The exposure for *Achillea millefolium* is a broad range, from sun to semi-shade.

Soil should be prepared as for a lawn, incorporating 2 to 3 inches of compost, and a supply of organic phosphorus (20 pounds per hundred square feet). If your soil is acidic, also include 5 pounds per hundred square feet of oyster shell.

Fall sowing of seeds is ideal, preferably done in September through October in microclimates where Indian summer slows the cooling of the soil. A half-pound of the fine seed is sufficient to cover 1000 square feet. If you are gardening in clay soils, do not mix sand with the seed. Large areas may be hydroseeded. Irrigate until germination. Established plants need little or no irrigation, depending on how lush you want your lawn to be.

BLOOM

If you mow this lawn area every few weeks in spring, there will be very few flowers, and those that do appear will probably be on soft, short stems to 6 inches. Taller stalks may, after mowing, leave stiff stubbles that are hard on bare feet. Allowed to bloom with little or no mowing, *Achillea millefolium* may have flowering stalks to 2 to 3 feet. Bloom is heaviest in early summer, and may continue through fall.

The cultivars of this perennial have a broad range of color, but all of them have been eaten occasionally by the deer in my garden. To establish a very attractive meadow, be adventuresome and try just a few of the red 'Paprika', darker red 'Cerise Queen', 'Salmon Beauty', or pink 'Rosea'. Perhaps the deer may not notice if they are growing among the less desirable white. Place those plants which will be allowed to bloom, and will not be mowed, around the fringes of your lawn area.

SEASONAL INTEREST

This lawn will be evergreen. Unmowed areas will bloom, creating a beautiful meadow in summer.

PROPAGATION:

Plants are easily propagated by divisions at any time of the year. If divisions are made in the heat of summer, cut the foliage back on each division by half to reduce transplant shock. *Achillea millefolium* may also be propagated by seed, saving seed from the flowerheads when they are brown.

MAINTENANCE

A lawn of *Achillea millefolium* may need to be mowed every three to four weeks if it is irrigated. Spring growth will be the strongest. If it is mowed a couple of times in spring, then allowed to rest through a dry summer, it may not need to be mowed again until next year. If you have allowed your meadow to bloom in early summer, mow after bloom, water deeply, then enjoy your lawn for the summer. If you are seed-saving, or want to have a few more flowers midsummer, leave the fringe area unmowed.

Achillea x 'Moonshine'
(moonshine yarrow)

One of the loveliest of yellows in the garden, this non-spreading yarrow has many wonderful uses. The silver-gray foliage is an accent for the border front, the flowers an extra bonus. Since each plant shows strong basal growth from the crown, and is evergreen (evergray!), use *Achillea* x 'Moonshine' as a single focal point, or cluster several for a grander display.

DESCRIPTION

Fern-like silvery leaves extend to 18 inches. Strong 18- to 24-inch stems support heads of bright yellow flowers for weeks. Shorter stems bringing repeat flowering later in the season may not be as tall or erect. The spread of a single plant is about 2 feet. Its deep roots reach for moisture, and lessen the irrigation requirements.

CULTURAL REQUIREMENTS

Zones 3–10. Keep this low-irrigation perennial in full sun for best performance.

Soil does not need to be amended with compost, but even yarrow appreciates some compost and rock powders (soft rock phosphate, and oystershell in acidic soils).

Adding 'Moonshine' yarrow to an irrigated border is tricky, but can be done if the soil drains easily and does not remain moist. Sometimes this is most easily accomplished by placing the plant at a dry edge where the sprinkler does not reach as easily, or on a mounded or sloped area in climates where summer rains are frequent.

BLOOM

Early to mid-summer, sulphur-yellow flowerheads may be as large as 4 inches across, with smaller clusters along the lower branches of the stem. Lovely in the light of the full moon! Individual flowers last for many days and fade slowly.

Pick at the height of the color for fresh cut flowers or everlastings. Repeat blooms in late summer, and even in fall may be smaller than the first show, but still bright enough to call attention to this rugged perennial. This year, one of my clients at a lower elevation (1500 feet) reported in late January that her 'Moonshine' yarrow was still blooming!

SEASONAL INTEREST

Achillea x 'Moonshine'

An evergreen (or evergray!) yarrow in mild climates, 'Moonshine' puts on its strongest growth in the spring, overshadowing the old leaves from last season. Early summer bloom is attractive with the greens of later bloomers, not yet showing their flower color. Faded bloom stalks are interesting in form and texture for many weeks. The foliage catches my eye during a walk through the winter landscape. A few flower stalks were dried and displayed in my grapevine wreath on the kitchen porch, and in my solarium display of grasses, seedheads, and dried flowers.

COMPANION PLANTS & LANDSCAPE USES

Blooming at the same time as early *Coreopsis,* these two glow with the first strong yellows in my sunrise border, where the early sun rising above the Sierras in the east lights the June garden. The silver-gray foliage and bright yellow flowers of 'Moonshine' also pair up nicely with feverfew (*Tanacetum parthenium*).

In my garden, golden feverfew (*Tanacetum parthenium* 'Aureum') is near *Achillea* x 'Moonshine', the latter in full summer sun, while the feverfew benefits from a little shade near a star magnolia (*Magnolia stellata*). This year, dark-purple bearded iris will be added near the yarrow, along my sunny dry driveway border. The blue-purple of the early-blooming bulb, grape hyacinth (*Muscari*), is a good spring focal point nestled near the foliage, where the silver hue heightens the blue.

In chosing companions, be careful not to overshadow this yarrow with neighboring plants that are too tall or aggressive. This silver plant needs full sun.

PROPAGATION

Make divisions during the winter months. Lift a mature plant with a fork, and pull apart the plant. Divisions are usually large, but easily handled without shock during the dormant season. Cut back all the foliage at replanting to encourage new growth. Occasionally my students have successfully rooted cuttings from late spring growth.

MAINTENANCE

Very EASY! Care for *Achillea* x 'Moonshine' is minimal. If early blooms are deadheaded, the bloom season will be extended. Removing the entire flowering stalk as it fades encourages late bloom even in the fall. But do nothing and the plant still looks great. Remove any yellowed foliage as it appears. This is usually an indication of overwatering. In winters of repeated snows, cut back all the foliage in February, stimulating beautiful new growth for spring.

ADENOPHORA

Adenophora confusa
(ladybells)

A lovely herbaceous perennial seldom seen in nurseries, *Adenophora confusa* is most often discovered in old gardens. This carefree perennial adds so much to the early and midsummer garden that it should be included in borders.

DESCRIPTION

With attractive basal leaves, and 2-foot stalks of delicate blue bell-shaped flowers in early summer, *Adenophora confusa* is a spreading plant that will not be invasive. In bloom its height is 2 to 3 feet. Soft medium-green leaves vary in size and are heart-shaped, to 3 to 4 inches in length. The leaves on the flower stalks are smaller and slightly drooping.

CULTURAL REQUIREMENTS

Zones 3–9. *Adenophora* will grow in the coldest regions of the western, northwestern, and southwestern United States, where snow cover does not always ensure winter protection from cold temperatures and wind.

Full sun to light shade is the best exposure for ladybells. In hot climates, protection from afternoon sun is important for extended bloom. Ladybells thrives in the filtered sunlight of a deciduous tree as long as there is no root competition. In cool coastal climates, ladybells does well in full sun with protection from wind.

Soil should have compost and organic phosphorus added, both for nutrients and to allow drainage. Winter wet will soon discourage this plant. A good organic mulch is important year-round.

Adenophora should be watered at least once every two weeks. In some coastal climates it will be drought-tolerant in semishade.

Ladybells does not tolerate competition with roots from other plants, and it does not like to have its own roots disturbed.

BLOOM

Blue bell-shaped flowers have a slight lavender cast. Each flowering stalk supports many nodding flowers. Protected from afternoon sun and heat, the flowers are long-lasting.

If individual faded blooms are removed, *Adenophora* will continue bloom over a longer period.

Ladybells is an excellent cut flower. Cut stalks in early morning and condition in warm water, as you would for any perennial. There may be slight wilting at first, but the stalks should recover and last well in a bouquet.

SEASONAL INTEREST

The broad, dark-green leaves form an attractive rosette in early spring. Stalks add a vertical interest as the plant begins to bloom, and the strong stalks of multiple blue flowers continue for weeks, adding color and form to the garden.

COMPANION PLANTS AND LANDSCAPE USE

Give *Adenophora* plenty of room to spread. It makes a stronger show in the border when there are several plants grouped together.

Companion plants should not be competitive. Clumping ornamental grasses such as the purple moor grass (*Molinia caerulea*) are compatible. A large grass such as Japanese forest grass (*Hakonechloa macra* 'Aureola') is lovely grown near ladybells, but keep it at least 5 feet away from your *Adenophora* planting.

A stand of the ladybells in bloom in front of Mexican orange (*Choisya ternata*) or box honeysuckle (*Lonicera nitida* 'Baggesen's Gold') is attractive.

In my garden, *Adenophora* is growing near golden feverfew (*Tanacetum parthenium* 'Aureum'), and *Liriope muscari* 'Silvery Sunproof', a striking combination.

PROPAGATION

While *Adenophora* roots resent disturbance, the gardener may lift and divide roots during the dormant season to propagate this plant. Remove roots from the edge of your planting, leaving most of the planted area untouched.

Vegetative cuttings may be taken in early spring before stalks elongate to bloom stage.

MAINTENANCE

Cut flowering stalks back to the crown when they are spent. Faded leaves may be removed as needed. It is important to renew a good organic mulch each year, with at least 2 inches of compost spread over the planting.

Alchemilla mollis
(lady's mantle)

After a rain, the leaves of *Alchemilla* magically hold water droplets, and hundreds of tiny jewels catch the light. While other plants in the garden dry out quickly, the hairy leaves of lady's mantle hold moisture, sometimes for hours.

DESCRIPTION

This herbaceous perennial has large (to 6 inches) gray-green leaves, with a silvery underside that creates a light rim around each leaf. Each compact plant reaches approximately 2 feet in spread and 1 foot in height. Sprays of tiny chartreuse flowers are born in abundance on 12- to 18-inch stems. Flowering sprays tend to fall forward, leaving the attractive foliage exposed.

CULTURAL REQUIREMENTS

Zones 3–9. Full sun in cool climates, and partial shade to full shade in hotter zones. Fertile soil and regular irrigation optimize this perennial's performance. Leaves will be larger and flowers more profuse if lady's mantle is not stressed by low irrigation. *Alchemilla* has self-sown in the compost under my nursery display benches, where it thrives with daily irrigation during our hot, dry summers. In my garden, where it has richer clay soil and irrigation only once a week, the plants are smaller but still quite beautiful.

BLOOM

Yellow-green flowers are very tiny, but add a lot of color to the garden in early summer. When needs are met, the show lasts for several weeks. Lady's mantle is an excellent cut flower, with strong stems, and it dries well. The flowers and smaller leaves are especially nice for pressed plant material, and what a pleasure it is to work with the delicate sprays in midwinter!

Deadhead *Alchemilla* only when you want the flowering material for bouquets. The airy sprays retain their integrity as the flowers fade. Many seeds are produced, and the following spring there are lots of volunteers if you let this plant self-sow on top of the compost mulch.

SEASONAL INTEREST

Although it is dormant in winter, this is a perennial with a long season of interest. Lady's mantle is very attractive the entire growing season from early spring to winter, with no grooming.

The flowers begin to open as the sprays elongate in spring. Color continues into mid-summer. Tiny seed pods are not showy, but do not detract from the overall appearance. Few perennials offer as beautiful foliage for so many months!

COMPANION PLANTS & LANDSCAPE USE

Planted in semishade near *Iris unguicularis*, *Alchemilla* and this companion offer interest in bloom and foliage. Single plants of each are perfect accents in a small garden space.

The yellow-green color of *Alchemilla* blossoms echoes the hue of wood spurge (*Euphorbia amygdaloides* var. *robbiae)* blooms, but don't let the latter overtake the former. *Iris unguicularis* might be a good barrier!

Alchemilla is an excellent edging plant, especially along a path or walkway. Plant at least one plant in an area where garden visitors will pause to enjoy the beauty when dew is on the leaves in early morning.

Lady's mantle becomes a focal point in the garden, spilling over a wall or walkway.

Any one of the hellebores (*Helleborus* sp.), each one with quite distinct foliage, may be planted in the semishade garden with lady's mantle.

One of my favorite companions is Japanese forest grass, *Hakonechloa macra* 'Aureola'. Both are dormant in winter, but what a show during the growing season! Also use the evergreen sweet flag (*Acorus gramineus* 'Ogon') with lady's mantle. Strikingly, the golden foliage of the two companions echoes the color of the Alchemilla flowers, brightening a semishade area.

In cool climates, where *Alchemilla* can be grown in more sun, grow it near a drift of yellow-flowering *Allium moly.* Lovely!

PROPAGATION

Easy from seed, allowing lady's mantle to self-sow will give you a more than ample supply of new plants. Mulch plants with a loose mix, such as compost, before the seeds mature and drop. Seeds are very tiny and must be sown on the surface to germinate. Fall mulching will usually prevent self-sowing.

MAINTENANCE

EASY! Even if you fail to do a midwinter cleaning up of decaying leaves, *Alchemilla* will look good the next season. Fresh new growth will simply cover the old from the previous year.

If you are a tidy gardener, at least wait until winter, when the plant is done with its show. Clean up spent foliage before new growth begins very early in spring, so that the somewhat fragile new shoots are not damaged as you work.

AMSONIA

Amsonia ciliata
(blue star)

A star it is! Beautiful foliage continues throughout the growing season, despite summer heat spells over 100°F! With slightly arching stems, the effect of the narrow dark-green leaves is graceful and strong. This herbaceous plant is attractive whether adding texture to the middle of the border or varying the height of the front.

DESCRIPTION

Amsonia is 2 to 3 feet in height and spread. Leaves are 2 to 4 inches long and willow-like. Stalks are arching, adding movement to the border with the slightest breeze.

The root crown of a mature plant is about one-third the width of the top growth. Allow space (2 to 3 feet) for the plant to show its full beauty. Deep-rooted, to 18 inches or more.

CULTURAL REQUIREMENTS

Zones 3–9. Full sun works in an irrigated border, where the plant can receive water once every 7 to 10 days during the heat of the summer. Afternoon shade means less watering.

Deep, fertile soil is ideal for *Amsonia*. The root system is strong, so try to plant it in an area where it can thrive for many years.

BLOOM

Lacy blue flowers in spring are attractive, but disappointingly short-lived. Their delicate beauty must be viewed up close! Do not deadhead the faded blooms: there's more delight to come with the seedpods.

SEASONAL INTEREST

In spring, the strong new shoots renew my gardening spirit. Early blooms need no attention when they fade, as the developing leaves soon cover them. While many other perennials put on a show, then fade, blue star keeps on going as the plant's foliage and form enhance the border. Toward the end of summer, the long, fine seed pods mature from green to light brown. In some falls, the foliage turns to a lovely golden. A spray picked as soon as the leaves turn may last for months indoors.

COMPANION PLANTS & LANDSCAPE USE

Wood spurge (*Euphorbia amygdaloides robbiae*) contrasts beautifully in form and foliage shape. Ornamental grasses nearby will echo the arching lines of *Amsonia*, creating a dominant mood of movement (especially when the wind blows!) and a focal area for fall.

Since the *Amsonia* foliage will die back in the winter, early-blooming bulbs (*Crocus, Galanthus, Muscari*) may be planted in drifts near the mature root crown for early spring bloom. Or *Viola odorata,* in some climates, will make a pretty evergreen ground cover with early bloom, and the *Amsonia* will shade the violets from the summer sun. Use snow-in-summer (*Cerastium tomentosum*) as a groundcover to drift through the *Amsonia*.

A single plant is showy. Foliage is healthy all the way to the base of the plant. Use *Amsonia* to define the end of a border, where rock steps or a path may lead to another garden room.

PROPAGATION

Blue star is easy from seed. This perennial self-sows prolifically! Spread compost around the plant in autumn, and let the seeds scatter where you want more plants. Lift the young volunteers before their roots grow too deep. But even a three-year-old plant is still easy to lift with a good garden fork during the dormant season.

Some of my students have also taken vegetative cuttings during the growing season. Early summer cuttings had roots within 6 weeks, providing plants for fall. Divisions are possible from mature plants. If you are sowing seed in a seed bed or containers, do not cover the seed.

MAINTENANCE

Very EASY! No deadheading of faded flowers. Winter cleanup after the stalks have collapsed is quickly accomplished by cutting back to the crown.

ANTHEMIS

Anthemis tinctoria
(gold marguerite)

A plant with a long history, *Anthemis tinctoria* was noted in 1561 in Europe. History is worth repeating. This is one of the best of the yellow daisies. In Filoli Gardens (Woodside, California), the cultivar 'Pale Moon' caught my eye. While the plants are a little rambunctious and undisciplined, the abundance of blooms more than makes up for their misbehavior. This is great plant for drought-tolerant gardens!

DESCRIPTION

The growth habit of this semi-evergreen perennial depends on how it's treated: with moderate fertility and irrigation, *Anthemis* is approximately 2 ft. tall and wide within two years of planting from a 1-gallon container. The more fertile the soil and the more it's irrigated, the more it sprawls. The root system is very strong. A more mature plant may have a wider spread.

The foliage is attractive, the finely divided leaves presenting a lacy appearance from early spring through fall. Crush a leaf to experience its pleasing herbal fragrance! It should make you think of chamomile, a close relative. *Anthemis* will be evergreen in mild climates, almost herbaceous in cold climates.

CULTURAL REQUIREMENTS

Zones 3–10. Full sun to very light shade is the best exposure. While *Anthemis* does not mind some competition from nearby plants, it should not be overshadowed. If it has to fight for sunlight, it won't bloom as much.

Keep your soil "lean" with the addition of one part compost to 3 parts native soil (clay or sand). Too much fertilizer or water will result in rampant growth. And it may be at the expense of flower production.

One of the best exposures in my foothill garden, where there is no summer rain, is full sun with a deep watering once every three weeks. Since my soil is clay loam, it holds water. Gardeners with sandy soils may have to water more often or mulch heavily during dry periods. Though some garden references advise alkaline soil, in my garden there has been no problem growing this undemanding perennial in acidic foothill soil (ph 6 to 6.5 after the addition of oyster shell).

BLOOM

Anthemis is an excellent cut flower with strong stems, and the plant blooms for many months, especially when it is deadheaded. 'Kelway's Variety' ('Kelwayi') is a bright yellow daisy and 'Pale Moon' a light yellow. This freely-blooming daisy begins in early summer, and may still be blooming in fall if its needs are met.

SEASONAL INTEREST

In my perennial garden, the early spring growth of Anthemis always catches my eye with its fine foliage. Because there will be so many flowers in the months ahead, do not hesitate to include that wonderful foliage and the tight buds in a spring bouquet. This delightful daisy makes a strong summer statement, blooming freely with little or no care. If it has been deadheaded, Anthemis may still be blooming for fall.

In mild-winter climates, the foliage may be evergreen, adding a bit of interest to the winter border.

COMPANION PLANTS & LANDSCAPE USES

Use this plant near the taller irises, such as *Iris spuria,* which has similar irrigation needs. The textural contrast between the two foliages is interesting. And the two plants make good neighbors, neither caring how much crowding the other does! They can even move a bit into each other's space and still get along.

Midrange in height, *Anthemis* may be placed as an edger. Its foliage is aromatic when brushed, so position it within reach of those who appreciate this attribute.

A small shrub such as a dwarf barberry (*Berberis* 'Crimson Pygmy') or dwarf spirea (*Spiraea japonica* 'Norman') is an attractive companion. The more structured form of these small shrubs offers a pleasing contrast to the loose growth habit of *Anthemis.*

PROPAGATION

Vegetative cuttings taken from side shoots during the growing season, from spring into fall, will root quickly. While even a mature plant will not give you many divisions, this is another way to increase your supply. Dig up a mature root while the plant is dormant, and with a sharp knife or shears cut rooted sections to be replanted.

MAINTENANCE

Deadheading extends the flowering season. This plant flowers so prolifically that its energy will soon be spent producing seeds if the faded blooms are not removed.

In winter, cut the plant back to its crown, or leave just a few inches. This is hard to do in mild climates, where it may be evergreen. But don't wait too long: new growth for the next season's bloom starts early.

Artemisia sp.
(wormwood & mugwort)

In a roomy, full-sun border, *Artemisia* adds light with its silver foliage, and a pleasing contrast to any other color. Care must be taken to choose the cultivar appropriate to your border. Some of these herbaceous wormwoods and mugworts are quite aggressive in their spread.

DESCRIPTION

Artemisia ludoviciana albula 'Silver King'

Artemisia frigida is an uncommon wormwood that should be included in more gardens. Commonly known as fringed wormwood, it is a plant 2 feet in height and spread. The long, delicate flowering stems have a draping effect, swaying with the slightest breeze. This is one wormwood that develops a strong crown, but is not invasive in spread.

Artemisia ludoviciana 'Silver Bouquet' is an aggressive spreader, and only for the gardener who is willing to spend the time removing unwanted stolons. It's worth the effort, since this *Artemisia* produces excellent material for bouquets over a very long season. This wormwood is 18 to 24 inches in height.

Artemisia ludoviciana albula 'Silver King' and 'Silver Queen' are cultivars 3 to 4 feet tall, that will spread as far as you give them room. They are a welcome addition to my dry garden, where there is plenty of space.

Artemisia lactiflora (white mugwort) has green foliage, and in bloom may reach 4 feet or more in height. One plant spotted in a Vancouver Island garden was 7 feet! In my hot-summer climate, it is best in partial shade, and always under 4 feet.

CULTURAL REQUIREMENTS

Zones 5–10. Full sun for all the species except *A. lactiflora,* which does well in partial shade.

Artemisia is a rugged perennial. In enriched soil, it may grow even larger than described, but wormwood will do quite well where soil fertility and irrigation are low. Add a little bit of compost to clay soil to get air to the root system, rather than to encourage rampant growth.

Overwatering an *Artemisia* will cause its foliage to yellow or rot. This symptom will first show up on the lower leaves. Plant *Artemisia* in a dry border or along a dry edge of the garden.

Artemisia lactiflora (white mugwort) is the only wormwood that may be grown successfully with more compost and higher irrigation (once a week in the heat of the summer). This green-leafed wormwood is also the only species that will tolerate part shade. In climates with hot, dry summers, *Artemisia lactiflora* prefers afternoon shade and more frequent irrigation (once a week deep watering).

BLOOM

The blooming species that have silver foliage all have insignificant yellow flowers. They are early to midsummer bloomers. Silver flower stalks bring texture to the border, especially the graceful stems of *Artemisia frigida.* All flower stalks have leaves, which add to their interest.

White mugwort (*Artemisia lactiflora*) has attractive sprays of white flowers in early summer. These are good cut flowers.

Cut stems of *Artemisia* 'Silver Bouquet' before it blooms to add a soft silver touch to spring arrangements.

Artemisia flower stalks may be dried for everlastings. Placed on a table to dry, they will not lose their arching form.

SEASONAL INTEREST

A long season of silver foliage, from early spring into winter, inspires me to include *Artemisia* in my garden. Sprays of *Artemisia* cultivars dried for winter arrangements extend the seasonal interest.

COMPANION PLANTS AND LANDSCAPE USE

Artemisia 'Powis Castle'

With mindful attention to their growing habits, include *Artemisia* with other strong perennials (*Achillea, Romneya, Penstemon, Iris spuria, Papaver orientale,* or *Origanum* species), or drought-tolerant subshrubs with dark-green or red foliage (dwarf *Mahonia* or *Berberis*).

A stand of *Artemisia* 'Silver Bouquet' catches the morning light along my driveway. Next to it, a clump of *Origanum laevigatum* contrasts with clusters of purple flowers in midsummer.

Drifts of *Artemisia frigida* soften a mugho pine (*Pinus mugo mugo*). With a backdrop of Matilija poppy (*Romneya coulteri*) and an accent of golden yarrow (*Achillea filipendulina* 'Coronation Gold'), this dry area of the garden offers year-round interest. Even when the selected plants are not in bloom, foliage contrasts are attractive.

PROPAGATION

Division is easy in fall, winter, or early spring if the *Artemisia* spreads by stolons or is a mature crown. If growth is still active when you are making divisions, cut it back to the crown.

MAINTENANCE

Herbaceous wormwoods and mugwort begin to die back as winter's chill increases. Cut them back to the crown, leaving no stems. In spring, the new growth will pop through your mulch as soon as the ground begins to warm.

Artemisia canescens (*A. versicolor*) is an excellent evergray edging plant.

Artemisia stellerana (beach wormwood) is the only wormwood that the deer have eaten in my garden.

Artemisia 'Powis Castle'
(also 'Powys Castle')

DESCRIPTION

Artemisia 'Powis Castle'

Artemisia 'Powis Castle' is my favorite tall wormwood. Unless it's kept trimmed, it can grow into a subshrub 5 feet (or more!) in width, so this plant is not for the small border. Easily maintained at a 2-foot height and 3-foot spread, 'Powys Castle' does not spread by runners into adjacent plants.

CULTURAL REQUIREMENTS

See *Artemisia sp.*, herbaceous perennials, above.

BLOOM

Artemisia 'Powis Castle' rarely blooms.

SEASONAL INTEREST

In mild-winter areas, *Artemisia* 'Powis Castle' is evergray. Even after heavy snow covers it for several days in my garden, this subshrub still looks good when the snow melts.

COMPANION PLANTS & LANDSCAPE USE

A single specimen of *Artemisia* 'Powis Castle' becomes a focal point in a dry corner where little else will grow. Using the fine feathery silver foliage of 'Powis Castle' to contrast with the dark green of upright rosemary *(Rosmarinus officinalis)*, provides pleasing structural and foliage contrast in the dry garden.

PROPAGATION

Artemisia 'Powis Castle' may be propagated by vegetative cuttings taken spring through fall. Sometimes branches will root-layer during the growing season. That is, they form roots where the branch lies on the ground. Cut off the branch from the parent plant, then make another cut to eliminate the top growth on the branch you have cut. The rooted portion may be planted for a new subshrub. To encourage this type of layering, spread compost thickly below a branch and anchor the branch into the compost with a landscape staple. Rooting should occur within a few weeks, and it doesn't hurt to pull the branch out of the compost to check it, as long as it is still attached to the "mother" plant.

MAINTENANCE

The evergray *Artemisia* 'Powis Castle' may be trimmed at any time of the year to maintain a desirable form and size.

Even if it has not been trimmed during the growing season, it should be pruned hard in late winter. Prune just before new growth starts in the spring, leaving about 12 to 18 inches of woody plant material, to reduce size. If an 18-inch high and wide subshrub is the end result of a winter pruning, the plant will be 3 to 4 feet the next growing season.

The later the pruning (February in my garden), the shorter the plant looks woody and barren. By early April, it looks lush and full even when winter weather has lingered.

Baptisia australis
(blue false indigo)

A legume, *Baptisia* has attractive blue flowers resembling pea blooms. Long-lived in the border as long as it has a sunny exposure, blue false indigo is a showy, upright herbaceous perennial with foliage that captures sunlight on its leaves. While a single specimen is interesting in a small garden, a group of *Baptisia* in the middle of the larger border will be a highlight for a long season.

DESCRIPTION

Baptisia is 2 to 3 feet in height. A mature plant has a root crown of about a foot and a spread at the top of about 2 to 3 feet. For the effect of a drift in a border, space plants 12 to 18 inches apart. Very deep-rooted, this perennial is difficult to move once established.

CULTURAL REQUIREMENTS

Zones 3–10. Full sun to very light shade. *Baptisia* performs well in strong light, and may even die out if overshadowed by adjacent shrubs or aggressive or taller perennials.

Good, deep garden soil, with oyster shell added if your soil is acidic, works best for this perennial. Soft rock phosphate should be incorporated into the soil to a depth of at least 12 inches, and even deeper is better!

Do not overwater in clay soil, but deep irrigation every week to ten days will keep this perennial performing. Lower irrigation (every 2 to 3 weeks) works, especially if the plant is well-mulched.

BLOOM

Blue pea-shaped flowers in racemes in late spring. Do not deadhead mature plants: the seedpods that follow are unusual!

This is also a good cut flower. You have to choose when the plant is young (1 to 2 years): a fleeting bouquet, or an everlasting? It's better to pick the flowers when a plant is young, so it will not put energy into seed production.

SEASONAL INTEREST

This is another herbaceous perennial that is a harbinger of spring, with all the promise the new growth heralds for another season in the garden. Each year, as the plant matures, more shoots come from the crown, promising sprays of exquisite flowers. In the fall, the seed pods turn a dark charcoal-brown. Pick sprays of the pods before winter moves in, to enjoy as an everlasting inside. Children love the rattle as they shake the pods. Of course, too much shaking and the pods may split open, revealing the golden-brown seeds. Seed—save if you want more plants.

COMPANION PLANTS & LANDSCAPE USE

Since the lower stems of *Baptisia* tend to be bare as the season progresses, team this plant with an ornamental grass or shorter perennial. The blue-green foliage and blue flowers of the *Baptisia* are wonderful color echoes with the silver-blue of fescues *(Festuca glauca* or *F. amethystina).* One of my favorite companions is *Penstemon campanulatus* 'Garnet' since there is a blue undertone to the garnet blooms. Bulbs and groundcovers recommended for combining with *Amsonia* would also work for blue false indigo.

PROPAGATION

Starting from seed, cover the seed with 1/8 inch of fine compost. For greatest success, use bottom heat in a cold frame. Young seedlings will grow quickly, but even with the best of growing conditions, it will take a few years before you have an established plant.

MAINTENANCE

Another easy-care perennial, the only attention *Baptisia* needs is to have the stalks cut all the way back to the crown of the plant when they fade at the beginning of winter. Do not leave any portion of the stalk, or it will be unsightly when the beautiful new shoots show in early spring.

Belamcanda chinensis
(blackberry lily)

An exciting plant for a long season, the origin of its common name, blackberry lily, does not unfold until after bloom, when the berry-like clusters of black seedpods appear.

DESCRIPTION

Height varies with soil fertility and irrigation, but 2 to 3 feet is an average height in my garden. When the plant reaches mature height for the season, the width at the top is about 18 to 24 inches, and at the base, 12 to 15 inches. The root is fibrous, and not very deep. The crown gets larger each year, promising more flowers, but this is not a spreading perennial.

With the appearance of bearded iris foliage, the light-green leaves of *Belamcanda* bring a strong, upright element to the border, which is attractive in the middle zone behind low edging plants. Or use this one as the edging plant where a border includes tall late-bloomers.

CULTURAL REQUIREMENTS

Zones 5–10. Full sun to light shade is ideal. Blackberry lily likes good garden loam and a regular supply of water every week. A thick organic mulch, 2 to 4 inches deep, is appropriate.

BLOOM

My garden includes two different colors of blackberry lily: orange flowers with dark splotches, and mauve blooms with similar markings. Hummingbirds check out both hues, returning often. The flowers are subtle, and must be viewed up close. Plant them near a bench in the garden. Blooming late summer, the flowering continues for a few weeks.

Blackberry lily is a good cut flower, and the stalks with seedpods like large blackberries are exquisite in dried arrangements. Dried material may last for several years.

SEASONAL INTEREST

Belamcanda is attractive throughout the growing season, beginning with the new foliage in spring. My favorite time to view this perennial is when the flower stalks begin unfolding like a ballet dancer, revealing buds on delicate stems. Soon the flowers follow, and then seedpods swell. As the seeds ripen, the green pod reveals the reason for the name, blackberry lily. Mature seeds are within clusters of black seedpods. At this stage it is difficult to decide whether to seed-save before winter storms scatter the promise of more plants, to cut the stalks for everlastings inside, or to prolong autumn in the garden by doing nothing.

COMPANION PLANTS & LANDSCAPE USES

Place this perennial where it will not be overshadowed by more aggressive perennials. The bladed foliage offers a pleasing contrast to many herbaceous perennials. Use it near peonies (*Paeonia*), allowing appropriate spacing for mature plants, since neither of these perennials should be disturbed by digging and moving.

Play with complementary colors in the border by pairing orange-flowering blackberry lily with the blue of *Caryopteris incana*. Color is fun: boldly place a container of orange blackberry lily near the mauve *Teucrium cossonii majoricum! Belamcanda* also works well with a drift of snow-in-summer (*Cerastium tomentosum*), for a long season contrast of light-green and silver. Dwarf shasta daisies (*Leucanthemum* x *superbum*) and willowleaf oxeye (*Buphthalmum salicifolium*) are good companions.

Place this herbaceous perennial where you will watch its changes. In my garden, it grows near an arched garden entry at the base of *Jasminum* x *stephanense*. Another *Belamcanda* grows in a container near a small table with chairs, outside the French doors opening from my bedroom. The flowers open as the morning light beckons them to a new day.

PROPAGATION

While this favorite perennial has rarely self-sown in my garden, it is easy to propagate from seed.

Belamcanda is interesting well into winter, even though the foliage starts to wither as the seedpods mature. Save a few of the clusters. In spring the pods may be opened to provide seed. Sow on loose compost, and barely cover the seed.

MAINTENANCE

EASY! Cut back faded foliage with fall or winter cleanup.

BUPHTHALMUM

Buphthalmum salicifolium
(willowleaf oxeye)

With its attractive growth habit and long season of bloom, this herbaceous perennial should be in more gardens. However, it is difficult to find in the nursery trade. Willowleaf oxeye, also known as yellow oxeye, was first discovered in Austria in 1759. A very vigorous perennial, *Buphthalmum* is seldom mentioned in perennial references.

DESCRIPTION

Buphthalmum saliclifolium is a showy perennial, 2 feet in height and spread, with bright yellow flowers. The medium-green leaves have a delicate appearance, but the stalks are quite strong and the plant does not need staking. If it arches, this is part of its lovely form. This is a good plant for attracting bees.

CULTURAL REQUIREMENTS

Zones 3–9. Willowleaf oxeye likes sun or light shade. In a hot climate, some afternoon shade, or the filtered sunlight on the south side of a deciduous tree, would be welcomed.

This is not a fussy perennial, though flowers will be larger in fertile soil in an irrigated border (once a week deep watering in my hot climate). In a cool climate, *Buphthalmum* will survive dry periods in the summer months. Acidic soils should have oyster shell added to raise the soil pH to 6.5.

BLOOM

Bright yellow daisies may be as large as 2 inches in diameter. In my hot climate in the Sierra Nevada foothills, they are slightly smaller. *Buphthalmum* blooms for several weeks, especially if deadheaded. The flowers are terminal, with a single flowerhead at the tip of each branched stem.

Yellow oxeye is an excellent cut flower, but with a short individual stem for each flower it's best used for small, delicate arrangements.

SEASONAL INTEREST

Because the plant is so attractive, yellow oxeye provides a long season of interest. Even when bloom has faded at the end of the summer, the plant still looks good. It is dormant in winter, but springs back to life as soon as the garden begins to warm.

COMPANION PLANTS AND LANDSCAPE USE

There are many uses for this wonderful plant in a small garden, a woodland garden, the larger herbaceous border, or in a container.

If you need a shorter perennial in front of taller plants such as *Baptisia, Helenium, Belamcanda* or *Amsonia,* this is a good choice. Plant a minimum of 3 feet away from taller perennials so they do not overshadow it when they mature.

A single plant along a garden path, or in a small garden, becomes a focal point when the yellow daisies brighten a sunny spot.

PROPAGATION

Buphthalmum can be divided before growth starts in the early spring in cold climates, or late fall in more mild zones. It may self-sow when seeds fall on the ground. In cold climates seed-save and try sowing seeds on the top of compost in early spring. The seedlings will be ready for transplanting to the garden in late summer or fall.

MAINTENANCE

Very EASY! Another carefree perennial, *Buphthalmum* needs little attention (other than to enjoy it!). Deadheading promotes more blooming. Remove faded stalks with winter cleanup.

Caryopteris clandonensis

Caryopteris clandonensis
(blue mist)

Blue mist is a perfect name for this attractive perennial subshrub. Drought-tolerant and late-flowering, *Caryopteris clandonensis* is an excellent deciduous subshrub for an herbaceous border.

DESCRIPTION

A single plant of *Caryopteris clandonensis* can get quite large. One specimen in my nursery display garden is 4 feet in height and width because it gets frequent irrigation, with excellent drainage. Growing in a low-irrigation border, blue mist is usually about 3 feet high and wide. Delicate clusters of blue flowers begin blooming midsummer and will continue into fall where temperatures are below 85°F in late summer. Leaves, too, are delicate and gray-green.

CULTURAL REQUIREMENTS

Zones 3–10. This perennial subshrub will grow in cold mountain regions of the western United States. Full sun is best for blue mist, although it will also perform well in the Sierra foothills with morning shade and full hot afternoon sun. In morning sun and afternoon shade, it may bloom less and the plant will not have as nice a form.

Add compost to clay or sandy soils for this undemanding perennial, but do not make the soil too rich. Irrigation may be as frequent as once a week, but this plant is very drought-tolerant. *Caryopteris* still does well with a deep soaking once every three weeks in clay loam, or every 2 weeks in sandy loam.

In cold regions it may be advisable to mulch the plants with straw for the winter.

BLOOM

Viewed through a lens, each tiny blue flower is extraordinary. Honeybees and bumblebees are very attracted to this blossom. Clustered together, the many flowers open in a wave of bloom. If flower clusters are removed as they fade, a second wave of bloom will follow. In areas with mild temperatures (below 85°F), *Caryopteris* will bloom for 2 months or longer.

There are several cultivars, each one with a different shade of blue, and a slight variation in size. All are excellent cut flowers. Use sprays of seedpods for winter bouquets.

SEASONAL INTEREST

As soon as its growth starts in early spring, this plant is notable for small, velvety, gray-green leaves. Attractive foliage is soon followed by buds for midsummer blooms.

With a very long bloom season, especially if it is deadheaded, *Caryopteris clandonensis* adds blue color for several weeks.

If later blooms are left on the plant as they fade, delicate light-brown seed pods will follow for fall and winter interest.

COMPANION PLANTS AND LANDSCAPE USE

Since blue mist does well in either the irrigated border or in the dry garden, there are many possible companions. One of my favorites is *Penstemon* 'Garnet', its later wave of bloom catching the first wave of the *Caryopteris*. The garnet-red of the *Penstemon* has blue undertones. *Achillea* 'Moonshine' and *Artemisia* 'Powis Castle' nearby complete a focal point of the dry garden.

Combine blue mist with ornamental grasses. The plant forms are complementary, with changing seasonal moods and colors from spring through fall.

If a taller accent plant is desirable in your rock garden, *Caryopteris clandonensis* is a good choice. It also works well for several years in a container.

Blue mist may be placed toward the front of a large herbaceous border, because its form and foliage are appealing. It may then easily be reached for deadheading, too. Attractive even when it is not deadheaded, especially for its late-season interest, *Caryopteris clandonensis* may also be placed out of reach in the middle or back of a border. It is attractive for the entire growing season.

Blue mist with dwarf barberry (*Berberis*) is a striking combination. The gray-green leaves against the dark red are enough of an accent in the garden. When the blue flowers open, it's an added bonus!

PROPAGATION

Vegetative cuttings from terminal buds must be taken in early spring before flower buds begin to form. Watch your cuttings closely, and remove any flower buds in the weeks after you have taken the cuttings. Cuttings root easily and will be ready for fall planting.

MAINTENANCE

This is another EASY perennial! The gardener can deadhead for extended bloom, or leave the faded flowers to form interesting seedpods. The only maintenance is a midwinter pruning, leaving just the lower woody growth with a few dormant buds. In very cold winter areas, mulch heavily with straw, and prune hard just before new growth starts in the spring.

Caryopteris incana
(common bluebeard, blue spiraea)

This exciting herbaceous perennial was discovered just a few years ago in a rare plant nursery. *Caryopteris incana* is now a favorite late-blooming blue flower in my garden. Even in the years following the death of my old dog, when several families of deer browsed in my garden day and night, this fall gem was left alone!

DESCRIPTION

The height and spread (and sprawl!) of *Caryopteris incana* varies considerably, depending on irrigation and soil fertility. An average would be 2 to 3 feet in both height and spread. Deep-blue flowers on this branching perennial are actually clusters of tiny blooms. Look at this one through a lens! The foliage is gray-green, rounded, with serrated edges, quite attractive during the growing season. Blue mist is an upright, bushy perennial, but will branch and sprawl where there is overhead irrigation and soil is fertile.

CULTURAL REQUIREMENTS

Zones 3–10. *Caryopteris* thrives in full sun. *Caryopteris incana* will grow in the coldest regions of the western, southwestern, and northwestern United States. Mountain gardeners should include this!

Light shade will work, but flowering may be diminished if the shade increases as the sun is lower in the fall, since maximum light is needed for lengthy bloom.

Caryopteris incana needs moderately fertile soil, and irrigation only once every two weeks in clay loam.

BLOOM

Deep-blue flower clusters with a hint of purple open for several weeks from late summer until frost, and the bees love it! This is a good cut flower and dries nicely. Cut flowers at the height of color for fresh or dried arrangements.

SEASONAL INTEREST

Late-bloomers look attractive all season, and this perennial is one of the best, with its gray-green toothed leaves and deep-blue flowers. A good landscape perennial for its form and texture, *Caryopteris incana* plays a strong role toward the front of the border, where one or more can be a focal point until the plant fades in winter. The clusters of blue flowers glow in the late summer and fall border. Bronzing of the gray-green leaves is a subtle color change noticed in late fall as the bloom wanes, so don't be too quick to cut this one back.

COMPANION PLANTS & LANDSCAPE USES

Because of its fall focus, this *Caryopteris* should be paired with ornamental grasses. A perfect companion, little bluestem (*Schizachyrium scoparium*) is a prairie grass that changes from blue to apricot as fall chill signals the gardener to slow activity and enjoy the transition. Planted near the dwarf maiden grass, *Miscanthus* 'Adagio', the textural contrasts between the grass and the broader foliage of blue mist is pleasing, and in late summer into fall, both plants are at their prime.

PROPAGATION

Take vegetative cuttings in early summer to encourage branching. Cuttings root easily, and will be ready for late summer and fall planting when taken in May. Hold off vegetative propagation by midsummer so that you will have lots of flowers.

MAINTENANCE

Flower clusters may be deadheaded, but it really is not necessary. In more mild climates, where fall is long and often warm with an extended Indian summer, deadheading the first blooms may increase the numbers of flowers. Cut the bloom stalk back to a bud that shows branching potential. Wait until the last hint of fall beauty fades in winter, then cut the plant back to the lowest buds (about 3 to 6 inches).

Catananche caerulea

Catananche caerulea
(cupid's dart)

When cupid's dart sways in a gentle breeze, its movement may call attention to an otherwise still border. Even without this visual quality, *Catananche caerulea* is a welcome addition in the early summer border because of its attractive sky-blue flowers.

DESCRIPTION

This is a small herbaceous perennial with long, narrow, gray-green leaves forming a mound. Very slender but strong stems support a multitude of blossoms, undaunted by summer rains, or even an occasional hailstorm. The mature plant is seldom more than 15 inches in width.

The mound of foliage is under a foot in height. The flower stems are usually more than 2 feet, each one supporting a single blossom. This plant may be semi-evergreen in mild winter areas where there is seldom a freeze.

CULTURAL REQUIREMENTS

Zones 4–10. Full sun to light shade. Give *Catananche* good garden soil, and you will be rewarded with lots of flowers.

Amend clay or sandy soils with compost, and add rock powders (soft rock phosphate and oyster shell).

Some garden references describe *Catananche* as "drought-tolerant", but my experience is that it needs irrigation once a week in clay loam in my hot, arid summer climate.

This perennial is a bit fussy about wet feet, and may die out in a few years in climates where rain is heavy in the winter and there is not good drainage. Remember that both soil texture and microclimate affect drainage.

BLOOM

Catananche caerulea has papery silver-blue bracts with a dark-blue center. The effect of each flowerhead is glowing blue. The cultivar 'Alba' is a silvery white. Each strong flowering stem produces a single blossom, each plant a multitude of stems, excellent for cutting. Bloom begins in early summer, and continues for 4 to 6 weeks, or longer. *Catananche* may still be blooming in October, even in hot climates.

Cut flowers are good for either fresh or dried arrangements. Cut the stems all the way back to the base since they will not branch to form more flowers. When cutting flowers for fresh or dried arrangements, remember to cut soon after the flower opens for the best color retention.

Deadheading helps prolong bloom of this perennial. If you want to seed-save, do not deadhead toward the end of the plant's blooming cycle.

SEASONAL INTEREST

While its bloom period is too short, cupid's dart adds an unusual color to the summer border. If no deadheading is done, the seedheads add texture through late summer. Remember to cut a few blooms for ever-lastings in the winter.

COMPANION PLANTS & LANDSCAPE USE

Although a single specimen can make a strong statement a small garden, if space allows, plant several plants to create a drift of flowers. The plant may not be as interesting as other plants in the border in late summer and fall, but in early to midsummer, the flowers are an exciting reminder of its worth. Grouping three or more plants close together simply increases the impact.

Using cupid's dart in the irrigated border, combine it with hardy geraniums *(Geranium)*, Santa Barbara daisy *(Erigeron)*, spurge *(Euphorbia x martinii)*, Siberian iris *(Iris sibirica)*, and indigo *(Baptisia)*. All of these perennials have similar requirements in exposure, soil preparation, and irrigation. And all offer nice contrasts and echoes in color.

Catananche is a delicate flower, contrasting exquisitely with bolder form and dark-green foliage, whether you use the blue or white flowering cultivar.

PROPAGATION

Make divisions in early fall or late spring. Dividing plants every three years may keep them vigorous, helping the plant last longer in the border. In ideal conditions, division may not be necessary. Fertile soil, plenty of sun, regular irrigation, and good winter drainage may help this perennial to live for many years.

Catananche is also very easy to propagate from seed, self-sowing in the border if you allow seedheads to develop. Or save some seed to sow in early fall or spring. Sow seeds on the soil surface, and do not cover them.

MAINTENANCE

Cut these plants back when they look untidy, or during your fall or winter cleanup.

Centaurea montana

Centaurea montana
(mountain bluet)

Related to the annual bachelor's buttons, mountain bluet is a handsome herbaceous plant, with a long bloom period, adding a strong blue accent to the late spring and early summer perennial border. Hot weather slows down the display, but doesn't discourage continued bloom. Butterflies are definitely drawn to this beauty!

DESCRIPTION

Centaurea montana may grow as tall as 2 to 3 feet in compost-enriched beds. In poor soils, it does not perform as well. A happy plant is lush and full, with large, dark-green leaves, and multiple stalks of blooms.

Placement 18 to 24 inches apart works well. Roots are strong and fleshy. The crown is about 10 inches in width, but will spread slightly by stolons.

CULTURAL REQUIREMENTS

Zones 3–10. Eastern exposure or light shade in hot climates works well. Full sun is an exposure that will work with weekly irrigation, or in cooler climates.

A wildflower, mountain bluet grows in unimproved clay or sandy soils. But its best show is where the soil is improved with compost and rock powders (soft rock phosphate and oyster shell). A thick mulch of compost around the base of the plant keeps the soil cool, and lengthens the early summer display.

Low irrigation produces a smaller plant and shorter season of bloom, while water every 7 to 10 days stimulates more growth and flowers.

BLOOM

The blossoms are delicate and intricate. This is an interesting flower to look at through a flower lens. Blue petals surround a center glowing with violet hues. Cut flowers are attractive in mixed bouquets. Bloom is strongest in late spring and early summer when multiple flowers open, attracting attention even from a distance.

SEASONAL INTEREST

This plant is most beautiful when late spring rains and mild temperatures have stimulated lush growth. Then the plant itself has a form unlike other perennials, almost as if a vase is holding it erect. In mid to late summer in a hot climate, mountain bluet wanes, though a few flowers may still appear. In cooler climates, *Centaurea montana* is a long bloomer.

COMPANION PLANTS & LANDSCAPE USES

A single plant is dramatic. Multiple plants (which you will have if you allow the seed to fall) are lovely.

Pair this one up with other early summer blues, *Baptisia* or *Amsonia*, for a color echo. The form and foliage of each is quite different.

Remember that green is a color too! The early spring growth of most perennials is exciting and not to be missed!

The silver foliage of *Artemisia* 'Powis Castle' is a beautiful contrast.

As the mountain bluet slows its growth and begins to bud, the foliage of *Belamcanda* nearby is pleasing. A color echo for that violet center might include an edging of late-blooming magenta violets. Germander (*Teucrium* x *lucidrys*) is a good companion with contrasting leaf size and form, and a color echo when bloom overlaps.

With a narrow crown, early-blooming bulbs (see *Amsonia*) in drifts nearby will be compatible with mountain bluet.

PROPAGATION

Centaurea montana self-sows, though seed clusters do not usually open until softened by fall and winter rains. Spread compost around the mature plant in early spring to provide a seedbed. Volunteer seedlings may be lifted and placed where you want them. A mature plant may also be divided, though leaving it undisturbed will allow the plant to develop a strong root system (each year gets better!).

MAINTENANCE

When the plant doesn't look good, cut it back to the crown. In my hot-summer climate, this is usually late July or early August. One June a hail storm destroyed the beautiful form of the plant, opening it in the center and bending over the stalks. It would still flower (lying on the ground!), but the form was ruined. There seemed to be nothing to do but cut the entire plant back severely and start over. Beauty is fleeting. The second growth was satisfying, but the plant was smaller, and there were fewer flowers.

If you are saving seed, first open a cluster to see if the seeds are mature (they will be dark and dry). Stalks with seed may be laid on the ground where you want volunteers to show next year. A more fastidious gardener will take the time to remove the pods from the stems and scatter the seeds. Cut all foliage back to the crown in late fall.

Ceratostigma plumbaginoides

CERATOSTIGMA

Ceratostigma plumbaginoides
(dwarf plumbago, leadwort)

Gardeners in the colder zones should try this hardier plumbago. While it is dwarf, it has the same beautiful blue flowers and red-leaf fall color of the more tender species. It is, however, very aggressive in its spreading habit, and should be placed carefully in a mixed herbaceous border.

DESCRIPTION

Dwarf plumbago is a herbaceous perennial under 15 inches in height in most garden soils. The richer the soil the taller it will grow. *Ceratostigma plumbaginoides* spreads quickly, forming a thick mat. New growth shows late in spring.

CULTURAL REQUIREMENTS

Zones 5–10. Dwarf plumbago will grow in any good garden soil in sun to light shade. This is a hardy perennial that will even tolerate afternoon sun in my foothill climate where summer temperatures can be over 100°F for several days. Exposure to adequate sunshine is important in the late summer and fall, for good bloom and leaf color change.

Gardeners in hot dry climates should give irrigation to this plant at least once every two weeks. In cooler climates, this plant can be drought-tolerant. In all climate situations mulch the plant heavily with good organic material.

BLOOM

Bright blue flowers in clusters provide color for several weeks beginning in midsummer and continuing through fall. The flowers are single, in clusters, and are under half an inch. Stems are long enough that this makes a good cut flower. Butterflies are attracted to this plant.

As blooms fade, the seedhead is attractive reddish-brown, lasting for several weeks.

SEASONAL INTEREST

With glossy green leaves on strong stems, the spring growth of *Ceratostigma plumbaginoides* is eye-catching. During the early summer before it starts to bloom it is an attractive addition to an herbaceous border.

In midsummer a few blooms open, and very soon the plant is in full bloom. As bloom begins to fade, the leaves begin to change color for fall. Even when leaves peak with their red coloration in fall, a few blue flowers may still be opening.

In my garden, heavy rains or snow will eventually end the seasonal interest.

Spring growth of dwarf plumbago is late to start. But the plant quickly catches up with other perennials in the herbaceous border.

COMPANION PLANTS & LANDSCAPE USE

Dwarf plumbago makes an excellent edging plant. Careful attention must be made to placement of *Ceratostigma plumbaginoides* in a mixed border, because of its strong growth habit. A few plants placed a foot apart will soon spread to cover several feet.

A single plant makes a nice accent in a rock garden or in a container.

Good fall-blooming companions include blue beard (*Caryopteris incana*), swamp sunflower (*Helianthus angustifolius*) and Santa Barbara daisy (*Erigeron karvinskianus*).

Plant dwarf plumbago at the base of taller ornamental grasses such as *Miscanthus* species or blue stem (*Schizachyrium scoparium*), or even the shorter feather grass (*Stipa tenuissima*). Grasses will hold their own, combined with this strong-growing herbaceous perennial.

PROPAGATION

Divisions of *Ceratostigma plumbaginoides* are easy in fall, winter, or early spring. If divisions are made in fall, the top growth of this growing season should be cut back. Gardeners in cold climates should wait until early spring to make divisions.

Vegetative cuttings from terminal growth root easily. Cuttings should be made from growth that is not coming into bloom. Most vegetative propagation is done in late spring or early summer. Dwarf plumbago roots quickly and will provide fall planting material.

MAINTENANCE

This is another very easy herbaceous perennial! Ceratostigma plumbaginoides needs no deadheading during the blooming season. During winter cleanup, cut stalks back to the ground. New growth starts in very late spring, so you can even procrastinate about winter cleanup.

Ceratostigma willmottianum
(Chinese plumbago)

In my Sierra foothill garden (Zone 8a), where winter temperatures can drop to 10°F in winter (with no snow cover), and summer temperatures soar to above 100°, Chinese plumbago is a good herbaceous perennial.

In the colder climates it will not overwinter. If you are uncertain about its survival in your climate, plant it in a protected location, and mulch heavily for the winter. In mildest climates (8b-9), Chinese plumbago is a subshrub, with new spring growth sprouting from the stems.

DESCRIPTION

Chinese plumbago matures to about 3 feet in height and spread. It is a gracefully beautiful plant with arching, reddish, twiggy stems. Late-blooming, its blue flowers continue into fall when the leaves are turning red. Even out of bloom, and with all the leaves gone, in winter this plant continues to be a valuable addition to the border. Though large, the overall effect of this plant is airy.

Roots are close to the soil surface.

CULTURAL REQUIREMENTS

Zones 6–9. Full sun to partial shade. Some sun in fall when the leaves are coloring is important.

Ceratostigma willmottianum

Ceratostigma willmottianum prefers a good garden soil, with compost and rock powders. If your soil is acidic, amend with oyster shell annually. Roots are very close to the soil surface, and will benefit as soon as irrigation or rain dissolves the amendment. Summer mulch is very important because of the surface roots.

To overwinter the Chinese plumbago, mulch heavily with straw around the base of the plant.

Because this is a long-lived perennial, and its roots should not be disturbed, attention to nutrients when it is planted is especially important. Though its roots are not deep, it does have a strong lateral root system (remember this when you're digging near it). Add plenty of compost, organic phosphorus, and oyster shell when preparing the soil. Mulch heavily with more compost.

Irrigate every 7 to 10 days in hot, arid summer climates. Where summer temperatures rarely rise above 85°F, *Ceratostigma willmottianum* in partial shade may need irrigation only once every three to four weeks.

BLOOM

Bright blue flowers open in terminal clusters beginning in late summer and extending into fall. The buds of the flowers have a nice reddish tone, adding to the interest of the plant. While the individual flowers are slightly over half an inch, and open in succession, their color is strong. Reddish-brown seedheads look like clusters of bristles. They last through the winter, even through snowstorms.

This is a good cut flower. And flowers attract butterflies.

SEASONAL INTEREST

This is a perennial that invites close inspection. In every stage of growth and bloom, it is colorful.

In spring, the new growth from the base quickly elongates and branches, adding both texture and form in the border. A mature plant produces a lot of flowers.

Ceratostigma willmottianum has one of the longest seasons of interest of any herbaceous perennial. Gardeners may leave it untouched until very earliest spring, when growth first starts to show at the base. All winter, the fine reddish-brown stems with their dried seed clusters move gracefully in the wind.

COMPANION PLANTS AND LANDSCAPE USE

In a large garden, a grouping of Chinese plumbago is striking. Place it in front of a larger ornamental grass such as *Miscanthus sinensis*. If you want an echo of blue, plant *Ceratostigma* near *Caryopteris incana*. They bloom at the same time, and both for 2 months or more.

Santa Barbara daisy (*Erigeron karvinskianus*) is a good companion, planted at the base of Chinese plumbago. The plumbago will arch gracefully over the Santa Barbara daisy, but will not overshadow it.

Early flowering bulbs such as *Crocus*, *Galanthus*, or *Scilla* make a charming display near the base of the *Ceratostigma*. Plant the bulbs 12 to 18 inches away from the plumbago, before its roots mature.

Place the Chinese plumbago where it will not be overshadowed by perennials with similar height. You want the full effects of the airy and graceful growth habit. Place it near a window for winter viewing!

PROPAGATION

Take vegetative cuttings from side shoots before the plant begins to form buds for flowering. This means that all cuttings will be taken in the early summer. They root quickly and will provide plants for fall planting. This perennial has never self-sown in my garden. Divisions are not recommended; the crown of the plant should be left alone to mature. This is a long-lived perennial.

MAINTENANCE

No maintenance is required until late winter or early spring, when stems should be cut all the way back to the crown. This is an undemanding perennial!

In my 8a zone, *Ceratostigma* showed a little growth from the past year's stems one spring, but it was not strong. Shoots at the crown showed more promise. While it is a subshrub in milder climates, in my foothill garden it is treated as an herbaceous perennial and cut to the crown in late winter. If it is a subshrub in your climate, you may cut it back to 12 inches in late winter.

Ceratostigma griffithii has an appearance similar to *Ceratostigma willmottianum*, but the deer ate it in my garden. It was moved to a garden with no deer, where it has thrived.

CHRYSOPSIS

Chrysopsis mariana
(Maryland aster)

A young visitor to my nursery was given the choice by his mother of a single perennial for his garden. *Chrysopsis mariana* was in bloom at the time in my garden, easily twice as tall as this budding gardener. He did not hesitate. The long sprays of gold flowers were irresistible. Butterflies, too, like this aster.

DESCRIPTION

This is the only aster the deer have left alone in my garden.

A rugged herbaceous perennial, *Chrysopsis mariana* does as well on the dry edges of my driveway (where it gets a good soaking once every couple of weeks) as it does in an irrigated herbaceous border. Maryland aster adds a strong yellow to my "sunrise border", a collection of warm colors.

A single mature plant has a base spread of about 18 to 24 inches, with long stalks arching to as much as 4 to 5 feet. Give this plant space! It's worth it. And while the deer eat most asters, they leave this one alone in my garden.

CULTURAL REQUIREMENTS

Zones 4–10. Full sun to very light shade. A wildflower in eastern states and Texas, this undemanding herbaceous perennial does well in clay or sandy soils with compost added. Somewhat drought-tolerant, Maryland aster will bloom longer if it has irrigation once a week. With a thick mulch the irrigation schedule may be extended to every 10 days to 14 days.

BLOOM

Flowers are bright yellow 1½-inch wide asters, borne in profusion in sprays along sturdy stalks. In my foothill garden, they begin blooming in midsummer and continue for weeks, complementing other yellows and golds which come and go. No deadheading is necessary.

After a few years of *Chrysopsis mariana* growing in my garden and nursery, a light yellow cultivar showed up as a volunteer seedling, and found a welcoming home in the border.

Chrysopsis mariana is a good cut flower, but removing stems will reduce the number of flowers. Cut sprays from inconspicuous places just as they come into bloom along the lower portion of the strong primary stem.

Fluffy light brown seed heads are also attractive mingled with flowers as the bloom season continues.

SEASONAL INTEREST

Maryland aster adds structure in the border with its strong growth in the spring and early summer. The foliage color is mid-green. Leaves are soft and slightly furry, definitely inviting to touch.

As stalks grow taller, they begin to arch slightly. As long as the plant has room and no overhead irrigation, it does not need to be staked since the stalks are quite sturdy. The arching form of the plant adds an attractive element to the border.

Bright yellow flowers last for weeks, and the seedheads add texture and color for fall. However, wind or rain may scatter the seeds in your garden.

COMPANION PLANTS AND LANDSCAPE USE

Because it needs no maintenance during the growing season, Maryland aster is a good perennial for the center of a wide herbaceous border. Or it might be a good selection in the back of the border, which may be difficult to reach during the growing season.

Companion plants may include other warm colors such as red, gold and even orange (yes, that one color that so many gardeners find difficult to use!). Planted near black-eyed Susan (*Rudbeckia fulgida* 'Goldsturm'), the yellow and gold are warm and sunny. But the two plants have strikingly different leaf forms and growth habit. And the dark seedheads of the *Rudbeckia* contrast nicely with the light-brown seed of the *Chrysopsis*. Watch for these details in contrast when you place these two perennials near each other.

The blue flowers of *Caryopteris incana* or *Ceratostigma willmottianum* are a terrific combination with the yellow of the Maryland aster. Pay attention to spacing requirements: be certain that each plant has what it requires for spread. This will be a focal point of the late summer border.

Both the green leaves and the yellow flowers of Maryland aster are nice combined with the red of barberry (*Berberis*).

PROPAGATION

Vegetative propagation may be done in spring, or by cuttings taken from lower stems even when the plant has begun its bloom period.

Easy from seed sown on the surface of compost, this perennial also self-sows in the garden.

Divisions may be made from the crown at any time the plant is dormant in winter. The entire root system does not need to be dug. Instead, use a sharp implement to separate small sections from the crown. In very cold climates, this method of propagation may have to wait until early spring.

MAINTENANCE

Another easy perennial, Maryland golden aster gets no maintenance in my garden during the growing season.

In late fall or winter, cut stalks back to the crown before new growth shows.

COREOPSIS

Coreopsis grandiflora, C. lanceolata
(lance-leaf tickseed)

Coreopsis verticillata 'Golden Showers'

A North American wildflower, *Coreopsis* is a beautiful addition to a meadow mix throughout the United States. There are several cultivars, extending the bloom from early summer into fall.

DESCRIPTION

Coreopsis grandiflora is the larger of these two plants, with the tendency to sprawl (as opposed to spread) to 3 to 4 feet. In its flowering stage, its height is about 3 feet. The cultivar 'Sunray' is more compact than the species with a 2½-foot height and an 18- to 24-inch spread. *Coreopsis lanceolata* has more basal foliage and may vary from 12 inches in height and spread, to a 2-foot height and spread. Size will always depend on soil fertility, as with most perennials.

CULTURAL REQUIREMENTS

Coreopsis lanceolata 'Brown Eyes'

Zones 5–10. Full sun to light shade.

Tickseed is tolerant of many soil types (sandy or clay), fertility levels, and variability in irrigation.

Coreopsis has a better growth habit if it is not in rich soil, but the addition of some compost will be beneficial. In addition to supplying nutrients in poor soils, compost has a great capability for absorbing moisture. Rich soil may result in rank growth.

Tickseed is considered to be drought-tolerant in many regions of the western United States. Loamy soils (clay or sand), and poor soils with compost added at preparation time will hold the most moisture for extended periods between irrigation or rain.

A mulch around the plants is a good garden practice to add nutrients and reduce evapotranspiration (loss of moisture due to wind and sun).

BLOOM

Large golden-yellow flowers (to 2 inches or larger) with multiple petals are typical of both these *Coreopsis*. Tickseed is the first to open of the summer golden blossoms, and 'Early Sunrise' is the earliest cultivar. If *Coreopsis* is deadheaded, the display of bright flowers will last for weeks. In mild summer areas where temperatures seldom rise above 85°F,

Coreopsis 'Sunray' begins bloom in June, and may still be flowering in September. In the Pacific Northwest, *Coreopsis* 'Brown Eyes' still flowers in October if it is deadheaded.

Strong stems support a single flower, making it a perfect cut flower.

SEASONAL INTEREST

Growth of the attractive leaves starts in very early spring, as soon as the soil begins to warm. Mid to dark-green leaves form a compact mound before stalks begin to form for flowers. In the mildest of climates, there may even be leaves during the winter.

Blooming for weeks from late spring through summer, and even into fall in some climates, *Coreopsis* is a "wave of gold" in the herbaceous border.

Seedheads are interesting, but allowing the plant to produce seeds may shorten its bloom season.

COMPANION PLANTS AND LANDSCAPE USE

Coreopsis verticillata 'Moonbeam'

Blanket flower (*Gaillardia grandiflora*) is a cheerful companion, beginning its bloom about the same time. The more compact cultivars of *Coreopsis* and *Gaillardia* may be planted 15 to 18 inches apart. If you have chosen larger tickseed or blanket flower species, plant them 2 to 3 feet apart, and let them sprawl together.

These broader-leafed *Coreopsis* will perform well in one of the most difficult of exposures in a hot climate: morning shade followed by full, hot afternoon sun. There are very few perennials that will thrive in western exposures in hot sun. In this challenging landscape situation, combine the *Coreopsis* with *Artemisia* 'Powis Castle', *Penstemon,* and *Gaillardia.*

Coreopsis next to a dwarf barberry (*Berberis*) or compact Oregon grape (*Mahonia aquifolium* 'Compacta') is an effective drought-tolerant planting for a small area.

Either single specimens, or a drift of multiple plants can be effective in the border. Smaller cultivars are good in containers.

Coreopsis lanceolata 'Brown Eyes' is small (under 18 inches) and compact, and may be used in a rock garden.

PROPAGATION

If you want to propagate a cultivar you already have in your garden, take divisions in late fall, winter, or early spring (depending on your climate).

Coreopsis is easy from seed, but seedlings from both species may be variable when you gather seed from your own garden. In a meadow, this is not a problem since any variation adds to the display.

Seed for specific cultivars may also be purchased from seed companies. Seed may be sown in late summer or fall in mild areas, and early spring in cold winter areas.

MAINTENANCE

Deadheading will extend the bloom season, but may be a daunting task if you have planted several plants.

Even as bloom ends, the plant is usually attractive. If you garden in areas where mildew might be a problem, remove the affected leaves or cut back the entire plant to stimulate new growth.

With winter cleanup, cut spent plants back to the crown.

Coreopsis verticillata
(threadleaf tickseed)

One of the most dependable herbaceous perennials for the border, *Coreopsis verticillata* adds much more than bright yellow blossoms in summer. Attractive and interesting foliage throughout the growing season are its greatest asset in a small or large garden.

DESCRIPTION

Each one of the cultivars of threadleaf tickseed has its own characteristics. 'Golden Showers' and 'Zagreb' are about 2½ feet tall depending on soil fertility. *Coreopsis* 'Zagreb' forms a clump about 2 feet in width, while 'Golden Showers' spreads even more. 'Moonbeam' is pale yellow and forms a mound that is under 18 inches in height with a 2- to 3-foot spread.

All have very fine bright green foliage, giving a delicate, airy appearance to the plant.

CULTURAL REQUIREMENTS

Zones 4–10. Full sun to very light shade.

Good fertile garden soil with plenty of compost will make this herbaceous perennial perform best. Keep it mulched and irrigate deeply once a week. Threadleaf tickseed is not as drought-tolerant as other species of *Coreopsis*.

Do not grow threadleaf tickseed in a western exposure (morning shade, then afternoon sun) in hot climates. The foliage will be alright, but the delicate flowers will suffer.

BLOOM

Starry, daisy flowers in abundance at the peak of bloom are 1½ to 2 inches wide. 'Zagreb' has golden yellow flowers and 1½-inch wide blooms, for a few weeks in early summer. 'Golden Showers' has the same size and color blossoms, but a longer bloom in my garden.

The pale-yellow flowers of *Coreopsis* 'Moonbeam' open in early July and continue until hard frost in October. This is the longest-blooming threadleaf tickseed.

A cultivar similar to 'Moonbeam' in growth habit, spotted in the gardens at the Seattle Center for Urban Horticulture, is 'Crème Brulée' with lemon-yellow flowers. It is in the "Blooms of Bressingham" perennial evaluation garden. While deer do not browse in this garden (according to local gardeners there are no deer around Lake Washington!), all the other cultivars of *Coreopsis* verticillata are deer-resistant, so gardeners in deer country may assume that this one is too. However, with such a delicious name it may not be!

Coreopsis verticillata is a good cut flower, and sprays of the foliage, when the plant is out of bloom, make a nice addition to a bouquet too. Stems are very strong.

SEASONAL INTEREST

Coreopsis verticillata 'Golden Showers'

The delicate appearance of *Coreopsis verticillata* makes it a beautiful plant in the garden at any time during the growing season. The flowers are an added attraction.

Seedheads are small, but interesting.

Depending on your climate, there may be fall color in the foliage before the plant wanes. In my garden, *Coreopsis* 'Zagreb' has attractive red tones in October.

Because it is herbaceous, there is no winter interest, but new growth starts very early in the spring as soil begins to warm. And even in a cold spring, the feathery foliage adds a lovely texture to the early border.

COMPANION PLANTS & LANDSCAPE USE

Coreopsis verticillata makes a wonderful companion plant with many other summer-blooming perennials requiring the same soil, irrigation, and sun exposure.

Paired with *Rudbeckia fulgida* 'Goldsturm', another plant with excellent foliage during the growing season, threadleaf tickseed offers contrasting foliage, form and flower size.

All three irises listed in this book are pleasing companions for the taller or shorter *Coreopsis verticillata*.

In using any of the *Coreopsis verticillata,* place them toward the front of the border to show off their fine foliage and form. The lower threadleaf tickseed are excellent edging plants.

In the rock garden, *Coreopsis verticillata* 'Moonbeam' is a long-blooming addition, but will need biweekly irrigation during a hot summer dry spell. The same cultivar in a container is an excellent accent plant that may be moved as needed to brighten a sunny spot when the color of other perennials is fading.

PROPAGATION

While *Coreopsis verticillata* will root easily from cuttings taken prior to the bloom, this will reduce the number of flowering stalks. Wait for late fall or winter, or even early spring, to make divisions. You can lift the entire plant, or leave the parent plant where it's planted, and cut into the crown to slip off a few divisions.

MAINTENANCE

Deadheading *Coreopsis verticillata* 'Golden Showers' may extend its bloom season. However, the seedheads on the taller cultivars of threadleaf tickseed add interest to the plant.

The long-blooming *Coreopsis* 'Moonbeam' will benefit from deadheading, but will continue blooming into fall even without this attention.

Coreopsis verticillata is herbaceous. Cut faded stalks back to the crown late fall or midwinter. Because growth starts so early in the spring, this maintenance needs to be done in winter, while the plant is dormant.

CROCOSMIA

Crocosmia x *crocosmiiflora*
(montbretia)

Crocosmia is an aggressively spreading herbaceous perennial with attractive iris-like foliage and showy flowers in the middle of summer. Hummingbirds love this colorful flower.

DESCRIPTION

Established clumps of montbretia are broad in their spread. The mid-green leaves are 2 to 3 feet long, and arching. The sprays of lily-like flowers of all the warm colors are held above the foliage.

CULTURAL REQUIREMENTS

Crocosmia x crocosmiiflora

Zones 5–9. Full sun to light shade is the optimal exposure. Montbretia is not a demanding perennial. It spreads freely even in poor soils. Adding compost and organic phosphorus will increase the flowering.

In climates where summer temperatures rarely get above 85°, *Crocosmia x crocosmiiflora* will grow in full sun with no irrigation.

The flowers will last longer if they are shaded from hot afternoon sun in most climates.

Irrigation once every two weeks in hot climates is enough, but montbretia will not mind being watered more frequently.

BLOOM

Crocosmia x crocosmiiflora has red-orange and yellow flowers, or solid colors of red, yellow, and gold.

Montbretia is strikingly beautiful in bud and in bloom, followed by wonderful seedpods. In all stages, sprays are attractive in flower arrangements. Cut sprays of seedpods (either immature or mature) for dry arrangements.

SEASONAL INTEREST

Because its foliage is so attractive, montbretia is an excellent perennial for the landscape. Its season of interest is long because the seedpods may be left on the plant through fall. *Crocosmia x crocosmiiflora* is dormant in winter.

COMPANION PLANTS AND LANDSCAPE USE

Companions need to be strong growers or sturdy shrubs. Planted near barberries (*Berberis sp.*), dwarf or tall, *Crocosmia x crocosmiiflora* is a striking contrast in color of foliage, leaf form and texture, and structure. When the warm colors of flowers open against the dark red of the barberry, this is a showy focal point in the garden.

Blanket flower (*Gaillardia*) has similar coloring and could be used nearby for a color echo.

For a complementary color, try blue *Caryopteris clandonensis,* a sturdy subshrub that will be undaunted with montbretia growing nearby.

In a small garden, grow *Crocosmia x crocosmiiflora* in a container to curb its spread. Plants in containers will need to be divided every other year and repotted in new soil to reinvigorate growth and increase flowering.

PROPAGATION

Montbretia is very easy to divide while it is dormant, or even after growth has begun in early spring. Lift clumps and pull them apart gently. Study the rooting system: it is both corms and stolons. Planted divisions should have roots, even if they are small, and will include both corms and stolons.

MAINTENANCE

No maintenance needs to be done during the growing season except to dig out spreading plants where they are not wanted. In mild climates, montbretia may need to be divided every few years to keep it blooming. Cut all foliage back to the crown during fall or winter cleanup.

Dicentra eximia

Dicentra eximia
(fringed bleeding heart, wild bleeding heart)

A favorite native of the western and northeastern United States, fringed bleeding heart is a perfect choice for dry shade. While it does die back when summer heat hits, so do other species of bleeding heart. *Dicentra formosa* is closely related and looks very similar, but is more tolerant of a little summer irrigation.

DESCRIPTION

A neatly mounded plant 12 to 18 inches in height, wild bleeding heart spreads to form large stands, dominant in the early spring landscape. When the snow melts, they grow very quickly, even in the shade in cold ground. The leaves are basal on strong stems, and finely-dissected, with a ferny appearance. The effect of the plant is very delicate and lush.

CULTURAL REQUIREMENTS

Zones 3–10. Filtered sunlight under deciduous trees, or even deeper shade from evergreens or a building. There is a beautiful stand of *Dicentra eximia* in the shade of my house on the north side.

Good humusy soil (compost, decomposing leaves) is desirable, and good drainage is necessary. Plants that are regularly irrigated during the summer months or in wet soils for extended periods may not survive.

In climates where there is coastal fog or lots of overcast days, this plant is more tolerant of sun.

This perennial is totally drought-tolerant! Do not give *Dicentra eximia* summer irrigation.

BLOOM

Nodding, pink heart-shaped flowers are held in loose panicles just above the leaves. On close inspection, each pink flower has reddish-purple tones. In my woodland garden, the length of the bloom period seems to be dependent on temperatures in the spring. The longer mild temperatures linger, the longer *Dicentra* blooms. A sudden hot spell over 80° may cut its bloom short.

Fringed bleeding heart is a nice cut flower.

SEASONAL INTEREST

Dicentra eximia is a beautiful perennial in spring and early summer. It dies back when summer heat begins.

COMPANION PLANTS AND LANDSCAPE USE

Use *Dicentra eximia* only in a dry shade or woodland garden. Combine with a planting of native ferns that tolerate summer drought, or lilies. A drift of wild bleeding heart in a stand of native deciduous trees is lovely.

A dry shady spot near a driveway, planted with *Dicentra eximia,* becomes a spring focal point. Add any spring-blooming bulbs nearby, and you have a new landscape that does not need summer irrigation.

PROPAGATION

Divide fringed bleeding heart when it is dormant. It may be divided as soon as the foliage begins to die back in the summer. Or mark the area where it is growing in the spring, and dig it as soon as rains have softened the soil in fall.

MAINTENANCE

No maintenance is necessary unless you are a tidy gardener who wants to clean up the decomposing foliage in midsummer. Remember that it might be better to leave it as part of the summer mulch!

Dicentra spectabilis
(bleeding heart)

Dicentra spectabilis

In a moist shade or woodland garden, late spring-blooming bleeding hearts are showy and unusual. While they die out soon after bloom is over, the elegant flowers are worth the fleeting show.

DESCRIPTION

The foliage is deeply cut and bright green on long stems, to a height of 18 inches. Each mature plant produces several leaf stalks, but it does not have the lush appearance of *Dicentra eximia*. Stalks of pink or white ('Alba') flowers are held above the foliage to as much as 2 feet.

CULTURAL REQUIREMENTS

Zones 3–10. Very intolerant of hot sun, this herbaceous perennial prefers part shade to full shade. Good rich garden soil stimulates a plant to produce more leaves and more flowering stems. An organic mulch is essential, and even a heavily mulched plant in clay loam will require deep irrigation at least once a week for best performance.

Leaves and flower stalks are fragile and should be in a protected spot away from winds.

BLOOM

Dicentra spectabilis

Heart-shaped pink flowers hang in a row on the stem, larger, to smaller at the tip. The cultivar 'Alba' has beautiful pure white flowers, a showy contrast with the rich green foliage. The show of pendant flowers lasts for only a few weeks in cool spring weather.

This is an excellent cut flower.

SEASONAL INTEREST

An herbaceous perennial, *Dicentra spectabilis* is a wonderful landscape plant, but fleeting. Perhaps it is because its time in the garden is so short, that it is so special!

COMPANION PLANTS AND LANDSCAPE USE

Place *Dicentra spectabilis* near spring bulbs such as the white summer snowflake (*Leucojum aestivum*), *Galanthus,* or species *Narcissus*. These bulbs will tolerate the irrigation that this bleeding heart requires.

Planted in a large container (5-gallon), *Dicentra spectabilis* will grow and flower beautifully. This allows the gardener to move it into the garden when it looks more beautiful, and hide it later where it can be watered but the yellowing foliage will be out of sight.

A grouping of *Dicentra spectabilis* may be over-planted with the annual or biennial forget-me-not *(Myosotis sylvatica)*. It will also push through the evergreen groundcover, *Lamium maculatum*.

Bleeding heart under small shade trees is a great combination. If your woodland garden is irrigated by late spring rains, this bleeding heart could be a good addition.

PROPAGATION

Mature plants may be divided.

MAINTENANCE

If *Dicentra spectabilis* is planted in forget-me-nots, or any groundcover, cut out stalks as soon as the leaves have yellowed. Otherwise no maintenance is required, and the withering stalks and leaves may be left on the ground as part of the mulch.

DIERAMA

Dierama pulcherrimum
(fairy wand, angel's fishing pole)

The magical names of angel's fishing pole and fairy wand reflect the ethereal qualities of this evergreen perennial from South Africa. While it is a perennial that will take up a lot of space, it's worth it, since it is attractive year-round.

DESCRIPTION

Very long, narrow, iris-like leaves have an upright, then arching growth habit. Height is usually 3 to 4 feet in colder climates, but may be more in mild winter areas. Spread of a mature plant may be as much as 4 to 5 feet, while the base of corms will be only about 2 to 3 feet in width. Blooming stalks add slightly to the height, and significantly to the spread. A mature plant in bloom may be as wide as 7 feet.

CULTURAL REQUIREMENTS

Dierama pulcherrimum

Zones 8–10. In the higher foothill regions (above 2500-foot elevation), plant *Dierama* in the warmest microclimates possible. In my garden at 2700-foot elevation, this lovely perennial has been slow to develop, and frequently struggles through the winter in my garden's cold microclimate at the base of Sonntag Hill. A few miles away, in the town center of Colfax, California, my demonstration garden has a large specimen. In this warm microclimate, it benefits from the slightly lower elevation and the warmth of the streets. In Seattle, at the Center for Urban Horticulture, there is a specimen of *Dierama* that is easily 7 feet (or more!) across in bloom. It is in an open courtyard, protected by buildings on all sides.

Full sun is the best exposure. Do not allow this plant to be overshadowed by taller perennials or shrubs planted too close.

Soil should be rich, with lots of compost and organic phosphorus, and a good mulch.

Irrigation should be regular, preferably every one to two weeks.

BLOOM

Very long, slender flowering stalks hold several pendulous bell-shaped flower clusters, 3 to 4 inches in length. Flowers may be lavender-pink, white, or mauve. *Dierama* blooms for a few weeks in midsummer.

Flowers do not need to be deadheaded, because the transition to seed stage is attractive. Or you may leave stalks on the plants through late summer or fall for their interesting texture.

Dierama may be used as a cut flower if you don't mind reducing your garden display.

SEASONAL INTEREST

Dierama is interesting all year! Out of bloom it is a beautiful evergreen when given the space it needs to be a focal point. Do not crowd it.

In bloom, *Dierama* is striking. Above the gracefully arching leaves, the "fairy wands" arch with their flowers, moving with slightest breeze.

COMPANION PLANTS AND LANDSCAPE USE

Dierama pulcherrimum

Nearby plants should be under 2 feet in height, and the closest should be planted 3 feet or more from the center of the *Dierama pulcherrimum*. Santa Barbara daisy (*Erigeron karvinskianus*), low-growing threadleaf coreopsis (*Coreopsis verticillata* 'Moonbeam'), or dwarf Shasta daisies (*Leucanthemum* x *superbum* 'Snow Lady') are effective companions grown near the base of the *Dierama*.

Larger plants should be kept at a respectful distance. When *Dierama* is in bloom, companion plants should not interfere with its form. Examine your garden for a special spot where *Dierama* can put on its show without getting in the way.

Angel's fishing pole is an accent plant, useful in a large container. Is there room to walk around it?

PROPAGATION

Corms of *Dierama pulcherrimum* may be divided during the winter, but it is best to leave the plants undisturbed. Seeds are easy to germinate, and this perennial may self-sow if there is open compost mulch where the seeds drop.

MAINTENANCE

Occasionally leaves will yellow, and dry, especially in the winter. These leaves may be removed individually by cutting them back as close as you can get to the crown. In colder microclimates, the entire plant may be cut back at the end of winter, before new growth begins.

The graceful flower stalks may be cut back to the crown at any time after bloom. Do not be in a hurry to do this since the seedpods are attractive too.

DIGITALIS

Digitalis lutea
(yellow foxglove, straw foxglove)

An evergreen perennial treasure for the irrigated shade or moist woodland garden, *Digitalis lutea* should be viewed closeup. The light-yellow flowers are pleasing in contrast to the dark-green, glossy leaves.

DESCRIPTION

Dark-green leaves, 6 to 12 inches long, emerge from the crown of the plant. Strong flower stalks 18 to 24 inches tall support several small, nodding, pale-yellow flowers. In all stages of growth, this is an attractive plant.

CULTURAL REQUIREMENTS

Zones 3–10. *Digitalis lutea* prefers partial shade to full shade. Plant in good rich garden soil with lots of compost added, and a mulch to retain moisture. Irrigate deeply once a week, especially in the heat of the summer.

BLOOM

Pale-yellow flowers bloom along a strong stalk, the lower blossoms opening first. The first flowers to open are about 1 inch in length, the subsequent flowers smaller. A healthy, mature plant will produce several flowering stalks. Bloom is in late spring and early summer, depending on your microclimate.

Digitalis lutea is an excellent cut flower, but don't cut every stalk if you want the plant to produce seed and self-sow. Deadhead if your plant is young so that energy will be put into growth, not seed production.

SEASONAL INTEREST

Straw foxglove is an outstanding perennial for the shade garden all year. Even when it is not in bloom, *Digitalis lutea* has dark-green rosettes of leaves, an attractive addition to the border.

COMPANION PLANTS AND LANDSCAPE USE

Do not allow larger shade perennials and subshrubs to overwhelm this delicate beauty. Use it near the front of the border or along a path where it may be viewed easily. Plant several *Digitalis lutea* for a stronger statement.

Planted near *Dicentra spectabilis,* straw foxglove becomes the focal point when the bleeding heart is fading.

Digitalis lutea is good combined with variegated ornamental grasses, such as Japanese forest grass (*Hakonechloa macra* 'Aureola') or purple moor grass (*Molinia caerulea*). Be attentive to the mature spread of each perennial when you are planning and planting. *Acorus gramineus* 'Ogon' is an evergreen with a color echo (yellow) of the straw foxglove flowers. Plant the miniature *Acorus g.* 'Pulsillus' in front of the *Digitalis lutea* for a sweet contrast.

Lonicera nitida 'Baggesen's Gold' would be a good nearby (but not too close!) companion, its golden-green foliage suggesting a color echo with the yellow foxglove.

Straw foxglove is also an attractive perennial for a container.

PROPAGATION

This evergreen perennial is easy from seed and may in fact self-sow if you have spread a nice mulch around the plants in fall or early spring. If you want to save seed, allow the seed to mature on the plant (always!). Remove a test pod and shake it on to your hand. Seed is very tiny and dark when it is mature. It may be stored for fall or spring sowing. Always sow the seed on top of the surface: it needs light to germinate.

Divisions may be made from mature plants if you don't mind disturbing this beautiful perennial. Make divisions during the winter or very early spring.

MAINTENANCE

EASY! Remove faded flower stalks or leaves as desired.

Digitalis x *mertonensis*
(strawberry foxglove)

Digitalis x *mertonensis* in bloom is a majestic evergreen perennial, towering over its neighboring perennials and even some small shrubs. A large display of strawberry foxglove is very striking in the woodland garden.

DESCRIPTION

In ideal growing conditions this foxglove develops a basal rosette of leaves, each leaf over 1 foot in length. Above the dark-green leaves, flower stalks may be as tall as 3 to 4 feet. A mature plant in spread is 24 to 30 inches. While the plant is evergreen in mild climates, in harsh winter conditions the leaves may not be attractive. In very cold climates, strawberry foxglove will die back in winter.

CULTURAL REQUIREMENTS

Zones 3–10. Partial shade will encourage the most bloom. *Digitalis* x *mertonensis* grown in deeper shade will produce fewer flowering stalks and they may be shorter. In hot climates it is very important for this plant to have afternoon shade.

Soil should be enriched with lots of compost and organic phosphorus. Add a mulch of at least 2 to 3 inches depth.

The irrigation should be regular and deep. Overhead irrigation should be avoided when the plant is in bloom. A good tree canopy over the strawberry foxglove will usually prevent damage from spring and early summer rains. Dry shade is an exposure that works in very cool and moist climates.

BLOOMS

The lovely rosy-pink, tubular flowers have interesting dark markings on the inside. Look at this one through a lens!

Multiple flowers open on strong stalks from the bottom up, the larger blossoms opening first. For bouquets, cut the stalks when the lowest flowers are in their prime.

For seed-saving, see propagation.

SEASONAL INTEREST

Digitalis x *mertonensis* is most attractive in early spring when the handsome leaves begin growing and soon form a striking rosette. Within a few weeks, flower stalks rise well above the basal leaves. Even before blooming, the swelling flower buds are fun to watch, and add a great texture to the border.

In bloom, in late spring and early summer, this showy plant is dynamic in the woodland garden or shady perennial border. With summer irrigation, the leaves continue to add rich green and lovely form to the garden for many weeks.

COMPANION PLANTS AND LANDSCAPE USE

Digitalis x *mertonensis* is a strong accent in the border. A single plant in a small garden adds a strong vertical interest in bloom, and a handsome perennial for the many weeks during which the plant itself is the focal point.

In a large woodland garden, plant a grouping of several plants for late spring and early summer display.

The vertical structure and pleasing color of the flower stalks is a good contrast to many shade-loving shrubs: sweet vanilla plant (*Sarcococca ruscifolia),* sweet daphne (*Daphne odora),* Mexican orange (*Choisya ternata),* variegated elderberry (*Sambucus nigra* 'Pulverulenta'), David's viburnum (*Viburnum davidii)* compact Oregon grape holly (*Mahonia aquifolium* 'Compacta'), or heavenly bamboo (*Nandina domestica).*

The large handsome leaves of *Digitalis* x *mertonensis* are striking with smaller-leafed perennial groundcovers growing nearby: Siberian bell-flower (*Campanula poscharskyana*), "dead" nettle (*Lamium maculatum*), sweet woodruff (*Galium odoratum*) variegated bugleweed (*Ajuga reptans* 'Tricolor'), or goutweed (*Aegopodium podagraria*). All three of these are strong groundcovers for shade, but the strawberry foxglove will not be overcome.

Biennial forget-me-not (*Myosotis sylvatica*) is an attractive companion with delicate sprays of pink, white, or blue flowers. This biennial is an enthusiastic self-sower and may not allow the strawberry foxglove to do the same.

Lady's mantle (*Alchemilla mollis*) and *Dicentra* are good companion plants. All of the variegated grasses mentioned for *Digitalis lutea* are also good companions, with nice foliage color contrast.

PROPAGATION

Digitalis x *mertonensis* is easy from seed and will even self-sow if the tiny seeds land on open compost and are not covered with falling leaves, or overshadowed by nearby plants. Not all the fading flowers need to be left to produce seed. A few pods will produce hundreds of seeds, but these seedpods must mature on the plant (this is true for all plants!).

MAINTENANCE

As flowers fade they may be removed, or cut back the entire stalk when flowering has ended. If you are saving seed, cut off the upper portion of the stalk, leaving just a few pods to mature. The plant does not need to put its energy into seed production from each one of the flowers.

Winter cleanup consists of removing leaves that are not attractive before growth begins again in late winter or early spring.

Digitalis ferruginea (rusty foxglove) is another perennial foxglove, grown for one season in the author's garden. Deer did not eat it.

Digitalis purpurea is a biennial foxglove, that self-sows readily. Seed in mid to late summer through fall in mild climates, or set out plants by the end of the summer. Deer do not eat this lovely foxglove, which has a wide array of colors.

Echinacea purpurea

ECHINACEA

Echinacea purpurea
(purple coneflower, hedgehog coneflower)

Purple coneflower is an herbaceous North American wildflower as beautiful in an herbaceous border as it is in a meadow. The flowerheads of all the cultivars are showy in size and form. *Echinacea* is a sturdy plant, undaunted by summer hail storms or wind.

DESCRIPTION

Most of the dark-green leaves are fairly large, and have a rather coarse appearance and texture. Sturdy stalks support large flowerheads. Height in good garden soil is 2 to 3 feet, with a spread of 18 to 24 inches in bloom stage. The fleshy roots are strong and fairly deep.

CULTURAL REQUIREMENTS

Good garden soil with compost added is appropriate for *Echinacea purpurea* to stimulate attractive growth and abundant flowering. Make sure that there is plenty of organic phosphorus available. Full sun is the best exposure, but purple coneflower will tolerate very light shade. Mulch heavily and irrigate deeply once a week.

BLOOM

The purple shades range in hue from rosy-pink to lighter pink. The center is dark with an orange cast. The first flowers to open tend to be the largest. There are also white cultivars, but the white is not as clear as that of the Shasta daisy.

Echinacea purpurea is an excellent cut flower. The seedheads make an interesting everlasting.

SEASONAL INTEREST

Purple coneflower is a handsome plant in the early spring border. In midsummer, very showy flowers add a few weeks of color, and even when they fade the plant still looks good.

In a mixed border, gardeners may want to leave the seedheads for interesting texture for late summer and early fall. Winter storms may end this display.

COMPANION PLANTS AND LANDSCAPE USE

Planted near *Coreopsis verticillata*, purple coneflower will contrast in both leaf form and color, and flower form and color. It is also striking combined with ornamental grasses.

Whether you use a single plant or a grouping of plants, the impact of *Echinacea purpurea* will be strong in a mixed border, both in foliage and flower.

Because *Echinacea* does not spread aggressively, spring-flowering bulbs that will tolerate some summer moisture may be planted close by (*Muscari, Allium, Leucojum*).

In a mixed border, place *Echinacea* so that it will not be overshadowed by taller perennials or subshrubs. Toward the front of the border is a good idea so that you can reach it for cutting flowers or early fall maintenance.

PROPAGATION

Divisions may be made by lifting the root and cutting into pieces of the crown, leaving a root section on each piece. This job should be done when the plant is dormant.

Gardeners may prefer to leave the root undisturbed, since it takes a few years for this plant to develop to maturity. Seed is not difficult to germinate. Sow on the surface of loose compost, covering the seeds very lightly. Late summer to fall is a good time to sow seeds in mild climates. Gardeners in cold winter areas may want to wait until early spring, so that tiny seedlings are not vulnerable in winter weather.

MAINTENANCE

Another easy perennial, *Echinacea purpurea* needs some maintenance during the growing season when leaves or fading flower stalks are unsightly, and should be removed. Cut all faded stalks and leaves back to the crown with fall or winter cleanup.

ECHINOPS

Echinops exaltatus
(globe thistle)

Many years ago, my garden had been open for a garden tour in which 500 people had wandered through over a period of two days. One visitor spotted globe thistle and observed that she was going to leave the wild thistles in her garden. *Echinops* is not your ordinary thistle! This one is welcome, but there are many thistles that are not.

DESCRIPTION

Globe thistle is 3 to 4 feet in height, with a 2 to 3-foot spread. The gray-green leaves are large and held erect. While similar to thistles (or artichokes!), they are not prickly. Round, blue clusters of flowers on strong stems are held above the foliage. *Echinops* is an herbaceous perennial.

CULTURAL REQUIREMENTS

Echinops exaltatus

Zones 3–9. Full sun is the best exposure.

Echinops does not need rich soil, but some compost and organic phosphorus will increase the number of blooms.

Globe thistle is drought-tolerant and also accepts regular irrigation in soil with good drainage. Leaves will turn yellow if the plant has been overwatered.

BLOOM

The blue flower clusters are the highlight of this plant, opening in succession for about 4 to 6 weeks. Since each flower lasts for at least two weeks, the total bloom period is two or more months. The blossoms are very rounded, an unusual shape. Each tiny flower is interesting to look at through a lens.

Globe thistle flowers are perfect for cutting, and also make a good everlasting. For either use, cut the flowers when the blue color first shows. Bees and butterflies are attracted to this flower.

SEASONAL INTEREST

Midsummer bloom is the strongest season of interest. If you remember to pick some of these flowers for everlastings, in the middle of winter you will be reminded of why you grow this perennial.

COMPANION PLANTS AND LANDSCAPE USE

Echinops is an interesting plant to use in a mixed herbaceous border. Its unique round flower shape and strong upright stems add strong vertical interest. With *Penstemon* 'Garnet' and *Tanacetum parthenium* nearby, the effect of globe thistle's foliage is muted. This combination of perennials should be watered every 10 days to 2 weeks in clay loam, or once a week in sandy loam.

Combined with golden yarrow (*Achillea filipendulina*) and Matilija poppy (*Romneya coulteri*), *Echinops* brings renewed interest to a rugged or wild garden. With mulch around these three plants, irrigation could be once every 3 to 4 weeks, or less.

Artemisia 'Powis Castle' is a very effective companion.

PROPAGATION

Make divisions of this plant while it is dormant. *Echinops* will self-sow, or you can seed-save and plant the seeds on top of your fall mulch. Gardeners in cold climates will want to wait until spring warmth to ensure germination.

MAINTENANCE

Cut *Echinops* back to the crown when its appearance bothers you. That will probably be right after bloom finishes. But if you are in a climate where *Echinops* looks good the entire growing season, no maintenance is needed until fall or winter cleanup.

ERIGERON

Erigeron karvinskianus
(Santa Barbara daisy, fleabane)

One of the most beautiful flowering edging plants, *Erigeron karvinskianus* tops the list of low-maintenance and long-flowering perennials. In my Sierra foothill garden, Santa Barbara daisy has bloomed for as long as eight months!

DESCRIPTION

A single plant will spread to about 2 feet with a height of 12 to 18 inches. Small, attractive mid-green leaves are quickly covered with an airy profusion of flowers, small white daisies with yellow centers. The overall effect is delicate.

Erigeron will be dormant in winter in cold climates. In my garden, it never dies back, but shows the stress of winter cold, and is not attractive in December and January.

CULTURAL REQUIREMENTS

Erigeron karvinskianus

Erigeron karvinskianus has done quite well in Sierra foothill gardens zone 8a (elevations 1700-3000 feet), where the winter temperature has dipped to 10°F, with no snow cover. One garden reference recommends this wonderful perennial for zones 5-7, another for zones 9-10 only. Try this in your garden!

Full sun to light shade is the ideal exposure. *Erigeron* is a good performer in coastal climates.

Santa Barbara daisy performs best in good soil, with compost and organic phosphorus added. While *Erigeron* is somewhat drought-tolerant, a deep irrigation every two weeks will keep it flowering. Mulch plants before they start growing in the spring.

BLOOM

Blossoms begin to open showing the rose underside of the petals. The effect of pink in the beginning transitions to white when the petals are fully open. 'Moorheimii' is a pale lavender cultivar, but the species, *Erigeron karvinskianus* is the most vigorous in my garden and nursery trial plantings.

Santa Barbara daisy does not need to be deadheaded. Bloom is continual from early spring until hard frost. Blossoms may be cut for miniature bouquets.

SEASONAL INTEREST

Santa Barbara daisy begins bloom early, late March in my garden. With no care, it blooms for many months, a profusion of rosy-pink and white blossoms.

COMPANION PLANTS AND LANDSCAPE USE

So many uses! *Erigeron karvinskianus* is an ideal edging plant and will tolerate irrigation once a week, yet still bloom happily if it is watered less frequently. Because Santa Barbara daisy continues to bloom while other perennials come and go, use it throughout the border edges.

A private garden on Vancouver Island, B.C., toured when the Perennial Plant Association held its annual symposium, planted Santa Barbara daisy between stepping stones. It was clipped to 2 to 3 inches in height, and was in full bloom.

My full-sun rock garden is irrigated every three weeks in the heat of the summer. Santa Barbara's daisy did not do well there, but along a dry garden edge with the irrigation once every two weeks it has thrived. With summer temperatures over 85°F, and several days of 100°F temperatures, *Erigeron* needs irrigation.

Delicate and beautiful in a container, *Erigeron* provides lasting color. This is a beautiful perennial spilling over a wall, or in a hanging basket.

PROPAGATION

Division is easy during the winter or early spring. Herbaceous cuttings taken during the spring growth root easily, but must be taken well before the plant begins to bloom. *Erigeron karvinskianus* also self-sows in my garden, providing an ample supply of young seedlings to move into other areas of the garden in spring.

MAINTENANCE

When bloom wanes, cut back all the season's growth. Set aside this plant material on a tarp. Spread compost where you want more plants, then shake the plant material you have cut and the tarp over this compost, scattering the seed. Then remove the spent plant material, and wait for nature to take care of the rest.

The plants that are cut back will grow quickly in very early spring. It's important to do your maintenance midwinter, before new growth begins at the crown.

The newly-seeded areas will provide young plants in the spring. These grow quickly, usually coming into bloom in the same season, but are not as large as mature plants.

EUPHORBIA

Euphorbia amygdaloides ssp. *robbiae*
(wood spurge, Mrs. Robb's bonnet)

Euphorbia amygdaloides ssp. *robbiae*

Euphorbia amygdaloides robbiae is one of the cultivars in this species that the deer have not eaten in my garden. A beautiful evergreen for dry shade, wood spurge is a focal point in my entry garden.

DESCRIPTION

A handsome plant with rosettes of dark-green leaves, this evergreen spurge grows 2 to 3 feet tall, and will spread from stolons. Out of bloom, it has the appearance of a small *Rhododendron*. With strong flower stalks, it may reach 3 to 4 feet in height in bloom.

CULTURAL REQUIREMENTS

Zones 6–10. *Euphorbia amygdaloides robbiae* does very well in dry shade, even in competition with tree roots, where irrigation may be as infrequent as every 2 to 3 weeks. Bright filtered sunlight is best.

Fertile garden soil results in the prettiest plant. Add 1/3 compost to 2/3 native soil, and an ample supply of soft rock phosphate. If your soil is acidic, also add oyster shell. Soil should not be rich, but the addition of compost and organic phosphorus will ensure a strong root system and drought-tolerance.

In hot sun, the foliage may burn unless irrigation is frequent. While this is a low-irrigation plant, it is tolerant of being watered.

BLOOM

Developing flowers are fun to watch in very early spring. When they rise above the dark-green foliage, they are curled tightly at the tip. As they lengthen, a slight curve is maintained until flowers begin to show. Individual flowers are yellow-green, and numerous along the stalk. When they fade, the stalks and the flowers turn to a nice light brown.

This is a wonderful cut flower, but be careful not to get the sap on your skin. To dry flowers let them mature on the plant, then cut the stalk in midsummer.

SEASONAL INTEREST

Euphorbia amygdaloides robbiae is a beautiful evergreen perennial, attractive in the border all year. Bloom begins in very early spring in my garden, usually while winter is still lingering with snowstorms. The development of the flower stalks takes several weeks. By early summer, the yellow-green flowers have faded to tan, a prelude of fall color.

With faded flower stalks removed by fall, this evergreen spurge accents the winter landscape.

COMPANION PLANTS AND LANDSCAPE USE

Because it is an aggressive spreader, companions must be very strong. In my shade entry garden, *Euphorbia amygdaloides robbiae* is planted next to sweet vanilla plant (*Sarcococca ruscifolia*) and paperbark maple (*Acer griseum).* When the wood spurge blossoms turn to light brown they are a color echo of the bark on the maple.

Maiden grass *(Miscanthus sinensis* 'Morning Light') is a strong ornamental grass, tolerant of light shade. The dark-green of *Euphorbia amygdaloides robbiae* is a striking contrast.

A large planting of this *Euphorbia* is perfect along stone steps on a hillside.

Box honeysuckle *(Lonicera nitida* 'Baggesen's Gold') is an ornamental shrub for shade that is a terrific companion. The small yellow-green leaves of the honeysuckle are a pleasing contrast with the larger dark-green leaves of the *Euphorbia.* Both plants are evergreen. In bloom, the yellow-green of the *Euphorbia* blossoms are a strong color echo.

Wood spurge is attractive in a container, but will have to be repotted after a couple of years because of its spreading habit.

PROPAGATION

Euphorbia amygdaloides ssp. *robbiae*

Euphorbia amygdaloides robbiae is easily propagated from rooted stolons lifted in fall, winter, or early spring. Vegetative cuttings taken from terminal buds when the plant is out of bloom also root easily. Always be careful to wear gloves when handling plant material from any *Euphorbia,* because it has a milky sap that may be irritating to your skin.

MAINTENANCE

EASY! Leave this plant alone to enjoy all its natural cycles. Remove spent flower stalks when they are no longer attractive. In my garden this is in late fall.

Euphorbia characias wulfenii has been tested in my garden for only one year. So far it has proven to be deer-resistant. This is a full-sun to light-shade perennial that gets very large (to 5 feet or more). It is not always herbaceous, but should be cut back to the crown each winter.

Euphorbia griffithii, E. amygdaloides 'Purpurea', and **E. dulcis 'Chameleon'** have been devoured by the deer! Too bad! They are beautiful species.

Euphorbia cyparissias
(cypress spurge)

Euphorbia cyparissias

Euphorbia cyparissias is a very showy herbaceous spurge, with fragrant chartreuse flowers in early spring. However, it is an extremely aggressive grower (invasive) and must be given its own space.

DESCRIPTION

With multiple very fine leaves on stalks to 18 inches, a bed of *Euphorbia cyparissias* resembles a forest of miniature cypress seedlings. When hundreds of fragrant flowers open in early spring, it is very beautiful and pleasing. Roots spread aggressively.

CULTURAL REQUIREMENTS

Zones 6–10. Full sun to very light shade.

Soil does not need to be rich, but should have compost and phosphorus added. A mulch will extend periods between waterings.

Euphorbia cyparissias is drought-tolerant. In full, hot summer sun in my rock garden, it is watered once every 3 weeks.

BLOOM

Umbel-like cymes (each main and secondary stem has a flower) of chartreuse blossoms with an intense sweet fragrance open in early spring. By April in my garden the flowers are glowing, more yellow than yellow-green at the height of color. Look closely as they fade: note the delicate shades of red-orange on the flowers. This will not be noticed from a distance.

The flowers in all stages make good cut flowers, but wear gloves when cutting to avoid the milky sap which may be irritating to your skin.

SEASONAL INTEREST

This herbaceous perennial is very pretty when it first comes up in the spring, and the foliage continues to be attractive all season long.

Glowing, bright, fragrant flowers are a highlight for more than three months in spring and early summer. Even as they fade they are still attractive.

COMPANION PLANTS AND LANDSCAPE USE

Dwarf barberry (*Berberis* 'Crimson Pygmy') is a good companion for this plant, its dark-red foliage contrasting with the soft blue-green of the spurge. In choosing companions, decide whether the invasive growth habit of the *Euphorbia cyparissias* will be a problem.

Spanish bluebells (*Hyacinthoides hispanica*) are bulbs that may be planted nearby in fall. If you allow it, the *Euphorbia cyparissias* will soon overtake the bluebells, but the *Hyacinthoides* will still come up in spring with their beautiful dark-green strappy leaves and clusters of blue bells. A nice contrast!

PROPAGATION

Divisions are easy while the plant is dormant. Vegetative cuttings may be made when growth first shows in early spring, or after bloom. Always wear latex gloves when handling any plant material from *Euphorbia,* including the roots.

MAINTENANCE

Very easy! In my rock garden this *Euphorbia* is rarely cut back even with winter cleanup. New growth in early spring quickly covers up faded dried stalks from the previous season since they are only a few inches high at the end of winter. Fussy gardeners should cut back faded stalks before new growth starts in spring.

Euphorbia x *martinii*
(spurge)

Euphorbia x *martinii*

A cross between *Euphorbia amygdaloides* and *E. characias,* this evergreen spurge is a subshrub that does not spread. A handsome plant, *Euphorbia* x *martinii* has many uses in a small or large landscape.

DESCRIPTION

Euphorbia x *martinii* is an attractive small evergreen shrub, new foliage with a red cast, mature leaves a rich gray-green. Spread and height are 2 to 3 feet, depending on soil fertility. Purchased plants may be variable in leaf color (see propagation notes below). This spurge flowers with stalks held above the foliage.

CULTURAL REQUIREMENTS

Zones 8–10. *Euphorbia* x *martinii* will not survive in the coldest mountain regions of the western United States, but it has survived ice storms in the Pacific Northwest, and winter temperatures to 10°F, with no snow cover.

This wonderful landscape plant may be used in full sun, in light shade, and even in deeper shade. Similar to other *Euphorbia*, clay or sandy soils should have a little compost and organic phosphorus added. Soil does not need to be rich with lots of compost.

Drought-tolerant, *Euphorbia* x *martinii* is tolerant of roots from trees and other shrubs. In this dry shade, irrigate deeply once every two weeks in the heat of the summer. Where there is no competition for moisture, water *Euphorbia* x *martinii* every three weeks. Water once a week in hot climates if you have planted this spurge in the sun.

BLOOM

Yellow-green flowers are typical of the spurges in form. They are small, clustered on strong stalks held above the foliage. The overall effect is a large flowerhead, called a cyme. Bloom is in early to midsummer in my garden, later than the other two species of *Euphorbia* mentioned.

Flowers may be cut for bouquets, but do not allow the milky sap to get on your skin.

SEASONAL INTEREST

Because it is an evergreen, *Euphorbia* x *martinii* is attractive and interesting all year. Flowers in early summer add textural interest and may be used for cut flowers. Use gloves so that the milky sap does not touch your skin. Dry the seedheads for a winter everlasting.

COMPANION PLANTS AND LANDSCAPE USE

This versatile evergreen is useful for small and large landscapes, in sun or shade, for irrigated or drought-tolerant plantings. Because it does not spread from stolons, *Euphorbia* x *martinii* may be planted near any other perennials compatible in soil, exposure, and irrigation requirements.

Strong foliage and compact growth habit make it a perfect companion with ornamental grasses, larger or smaller. In partial shade, pair this spurge with *Miscanthus sinensis* 'Morning Light' or *Molinia caerulea*. Be attentive to the eventual spread of each plant selected. Do not crowd these beauties.

Euphorbia x *martinii* is very attractive with drifts of spring-blooming bulbs nearby. Or try this spurge in a large container for a handsome accent plant.

PROPAGATION

Using latex gloves, make vegetative cuttings during the growing season when the plant is not in bloom. *Euphorbia* x *martinii* when purchased may be variable. Select the color of leaf that you prefer for your garden. Divisions do not work with this plant because it does not spread aggressively. Leave the established crown alone.

MAINTENANCE

Very EASY! Just remove the faded flower stalks when they are no longer attractive. Older plants may be reinvigorated with a light pruning in early spring.

GAILLARDIA

Gaillardia grandiflora
(blanket flower)

An enthusiastic bloomer with colorful flowerheads from early summer until frost, *Gaillardia grandiflora* is a dependable herbaceous perennial. In the warmest climates, it may be evergreen. There are compact cultivars that are best for the rock garden and larger cultivars for the mixed border.

DESCRIPTION

Gaillardia grandiflora branches freely, with multiple flowerheads on a plant that sprawls to 3 or more feet. Height depends on whether the plant is held upright by neighboring plants. It may vary from 18 inches to 3 feet. Allow for a 3-foot spread. Foliage is an attractive gray-green.

The dwarf cultivar of this plant, 'Goblin', is very compact with a 12- to 18-inch height and spread.

CULTURAL REQUIREMENTS

Zones 3–10. The best exposure is full sun to light shade, but this perennial grows well and blooms well with just a half-day of sun. And it is one of the few plants that will take morning shade followed by western sun in a hot climate.

These vigorous plants are not fussy about soil. *Gaillardia grandiflora* will bloom longer if compost and organic phosphorus are added. Gardeners with clay soil should definitely lighten their soil with compost to ensure that this perennial lasts for years in their garden. Wet, heavy soils in winter are not good for blanket flower.

Blanket flower is very drought-tolerant but will also accept irrigation. Planted in good soil with compost and mulch added, *Gaillardia* may be watered as infrequently as once every 2 to 3 weeks in hot climates. Gardeners in cool climates may not have to water this strong perennial at all in the heat of the summer.

Overhead watering or summer rain does not seem to injure *Gaillardia*.

BLOOM

This is another lovely daisy for the perennial border. The warm colors of orange, red, and gold may not be for every gardener's taste, but there are few perennials as abundant in flowering!

The color range varies: 'Burgundy' is a deep red, 'Yellow Queen' is a solid yellow, and 'Monarch' is a mix of all the warm colors.

'Goblin' has short flower stems in a blend of warm colors on a very compact plant.

The larger cultivars have long stems, making them ideal for cut flowers. Immature seedheads make good everlastings when they are cut and dried.

Bloom continues for months, especially when the plant is deadheaded. It begins in early spring and continues until very hard frost.

SEASONAL INTEREST

Because of its long bloom, *Gaillardia* is a wonderful addition to the garden. Faded flowers add a textural interest as they transition to seedheads.

Deadheading faded flowers will ensure many more blooms from early spring until hard frost. Leave just a few for added textural interest. A single seedhead will provide an ample supply of seeds.

There's no winter interest unless you have picked some of those immature seedheads (while they are still reddish) for everlasting bouquets.

COMPANION PLANTS AND LANDSCAPE USE

Gaillardia grandiflora

Anthemis tinctoria is a terrific companion for the larger *Gaillardia* because it, too, blooms freely for many weeks. Both plants have a sprawling habit, and will mingle happily given the space.

For a complementary color combination plant the *Gaillardia grandiflora* near *Caryopteris.*

Combined with the strong foliage of *Iris spuria,* blanket flower will be held upright, its warm flowers a beautiful contrast to the iris foliage.

In the dry garden, combine *Gaillardia* with species daffodils, planting the bulbs a minimum of 2 feet away from the crown(s) of the blanket flower. The dark-green foliage of the bulbs is an attractive contrast with the gray-green foliage of the blanket flower. The *Gaillardia* will soon sprawl over the spent bulb foliage. Bulbs will continue to come up year after year as they multiply around mature *Gaillardia* plants.

Purple *Allium* blooms at the same time, and is an exciting companion. Add *Artemisia* 'Powis Castle' and let the *Gaillardia* ramble through its silver foliage.

PROPAGATION

Gaillardia is so easy from seed that there is little reason to disturb mature plants for divisions, though that will also work to increase plantings. This plant will self-sow. If you are sowing seed, press the seed into compost, or cover very lightly. It germinates easily in spring, summer or early fall.

MAINTENANCE

Clean up the plant in winter, removing all the spent foliage and stalks. Gardeners in mild climates may be tempted to leave more than they should because the plant is semi-evergreen. In this case, leave only a few leaves around the crown of the plant. This will stimulate new growth and the plant will be much more attractive in the coming season.

Deadheading is advised. If blanket flower produces lots of seedheads, flowering will slow.

GALIUM

Galium odoratum
(sweet woodruff)

A wonderful perennial to mingle with other plants in the woodland garden or any border, *Galium odoratum* is most often seen used as a groundcover in the landscape. Sweet woodruff is a very delicate plant in appearance, but a strong grower.

DESCRIPTION

Galium odoratum is an herbaceous perennial spreading from stolons. Small mid-green leaves and tiny white flowers in sprays give this plant an airy appearance. It is from 12 to 18 inches in height in bloom, and will spread as far as you give it room in good soil.

CULTURAL REQUIREMENTS

Zones 5-8. Best shaded from hot afternoon sun, *Galium odoratum* will perform well in full morning sun or filtered sunlight under trees.

Soil should be enriched with compost and organic phosphorus and a good mulch. Sweet woodruff is not fussy about soil but is certainly more lush and attractive when grown in good soil.

Galium odoratum should be watered deeply once a week. In dry shade its growth will be very sparse, but still attractive.

BLOOM

Galium odoratum

Clusters of tiny, white flowers for several weeks in spring, open in sprays held well above the foliage. A mass of *Galium odoratum* is a beautiful sight.

There's no need to deadhead this plant, but do cut sprays for bouquets. The leaves, fresh or dried, have a wonderful fragrance.

If early summer temperatures are cool, this plant will continue to bloom until heat begins. In mild summer temperatures, below 85°F, sweet woodruff may continue to bloom until fall.

SEASONAL INTEREST

Galium odoratum begins growth very early in the spring. At every stage, sweet woodruff has such a delicate, airy appearance, that it is very attractive in the garden. Even when bloom fades, it needs no attention and continues to look good until hard frost.

Sweet woodruff is dormant in winter, except in the mildest climates.

COMPANION PLANTS AND LANDSCAPE USE

The contrast with the foliage of *Alchemilla mollis* is pleasing in a semi-shade border. Companions and landscape use for *Alchemilla mollis* also work well with this plant.

While the growth habit of sweet woodruff is very aggressive, it is easy to pull out plants where they are not wanted.

Use *Galium odoratum* as a ground cover, as an accent against bolder leaves, or even as a container plant.

Summer snowflake (*Leucojum aestivum*) is a bulb that looks striking in a bed of Galium, its dark-green, strappy leaves contrasting with the delicate whorls of light-green of the *Galium* leaves. In some climates they will bloom at the same time and, although they are both white, it is the color and form of leaves that offer the strength of contrasts. And even the small delicate white flowers of the *Galium,* in contrast with the bell-shaped flowers of the *Leucojum,* is pleasing. Some of the best details in a garden are the finest and most subtle.

PROPAGATION

Division, done during the dormant season, is the easiest way to propagate *Galium.* Lift sections of the plant with a fork and pull apart clumps. If any foliage remains, cut this back to the crown of the plant.

However, you may not want to disturb the plant in the garden. Vegetative cuttings taken during the growing season from terminal buds with no flowering stems, will root quickly and provide planting material for fall.

MAINTENANCE

This lovely plant is EASY! Winter cleanup is all that will need to be done in most climates. In the woodland garden, no maintenance is necessary. The new growth in spring will come up through the old, faded plant material from last season.

In the maintained garden, cut all spent foliage and flower stalks back to the crown of the plant, and spread a new mulch. Remember that the growth starts very early in the spring, so this task will need to be done in midwinter or late fall.

If you garden in a very long growing season, and *Galium* begins to look spent in the middle of the summer, cut it back to encourage new growth.

Geranium x oxianum 'Claridge Druce'

GERANIUM

Hardy cranesbills are beautiful herbaceous perennials planted in the right exposure! The *Geranium* genus includes many species with different colors and growth habits. Not all are deer-resistant, but here are a few that have been successful in my garden.

Geranium x cantabrigiense

This robust species has been the best performer in my Sierra foothill garden, where summer heat and very low humidity challenge this gardener and her plants in midsummer.

DESCRIPTION

This herbaceous cranesbill forms an attractive clump with delicate, pink flowers held above the foliage. Its height is about 15 to 18 inches, with the spread of a mature plant to 2 feet. The cultivar 'Biokovo' is under a foot in height with an 18-inch spread. Both plants have foliage that has a wonderful fragrance, unusual in the *Geranium* genus. Perhaps the deer leave it alone because of this!

CULTURAL REQUIREMENTS

Geranium sanguineum 'Cedric Morris'

Zones 5–10. In my hot garden at 2700-foot elevation, cranesbill is planted in semi-shade, in filtered sunlight or full afternoon shade. In the cooler regions of zone 8a, at higher elevations or in cooler microclimates, *Geranium x cantabrigiense* may be planted in a sunny location, or in bright shade.

Soil should be in good tilth for this plant. Add plenty of compost and organic phosphorus and a generous mulch that is renewed each year.

Irrigation should be deep and frequent in hot climates. Once a week is essential in the summer heat. In coastal climates, *Geranium x cantabrigiense* is fairly drought-tolerant in partial shade with a good mulch.

BLOOM

The flowers of *Geranium x cantabrigiense* are very delicate in appearance. Dainty, pale-pink blooms are held above the foliage on strong stems. The flowering begins in May in my garden and will continue into early summer if temperatures are cool, and deadheading is done. Gardeners in cooler climates may enjoy this plant in bloom for most of the summer.

This is a pretty cut flower, but does not last long in a bouquet.

SEASONAL INTEREST

The very attractive foliage adds beauty to the landscape from early spring until winter. Flowers are an added bonus in late spring into summer.

COMPANION PLANTS AND LANDSCAPE USE

As a semi-shade plant, cranesbill enjoys the same companion plants and landscape uses as *Alchemilla mollis*.

Use either 'Biokovo' or the species as an edging along a walkway and plan to brush up against it, releasing that wonderful fragrance of the foliage.

This is an attractive plant in a container. In a semi-shade rock garden or small garden, a single *Geranium* x *cantabrigiense* plant would be a good accent.

PROPAGATION

Because this cranesbill is a sterile hybrid, propagation must be by divisions, made very easily when the plant is dormant. With a mature clump, dig into the back side (leave the front facing the border or edge undisturbed), and remove one small section. This may be made into several divisions, each with its own root system.

MAINTENANCE

EASY! Winter cleanup consists of removing spent stalks and leaves, cutting them back to the crown. Deadhead to extend the flowering season. Renew your mulch each winter.

Geranium sanguinium
(bloody cranesbill)

Geranium sanguinium 'Cedric Morris' has been splendid in my garden, weaving through taller plants, but never a nuisance. It is herbaceous.

DESCRIPTION

'Cedric Morris' branches freely, sprawling on the ground, mingling with taller neighbors, or even accenting a small area with its 18 to 24-inch spread and 6-inch height. Finely divided, mid-green leaves are attractive texture and color in the front of the border.

CULTURAL REQUIREMENTS

Similar to *Geranium* x *cantabrigiense,* but this cultivar of *Geranium sanguinium* tolerates more sun in my garden. Perhaps this is because of taller perennials nearby which shade it a bit.

BLOOM

Blooms are 1 inch wide, a very bright, deep-pink. Flowering begins in early summer and continues for several weeks even when plants are not deadheaded. Stems are too short for cutting, but a branching section of leaves and blooms may be cut, which will encourage even more branching and blooming. As a cut flower it does not last long.

COMPANION PLANTS AND LANDSCAPE USE

Geranium 'Cedric Morris' echoes the deep magenta flowers of *Lychnis coronaria* when they are planted near each other. The lacy foliage contrasts with the gray leaves of the *Lychnis.* And both will do well in light shade and with moderate irrigation.

Use this wonderful perennial freely in your herbaceous border, especially where you have planted blues, pinks, purples, and whites. 'Cedric Morris' is a pleasing companion with all of these colors. Placed toward the front of the border, it will mingle with other plants without overshadowing them.

PROPAGATION

Divisions are easy to make during the dormant season. This wonderful perennial also self-sows occasionally in my garden. Vegetative cuttings may be made from terminal growth before or after bloom.

MAINTENANCE

Very EASY! This plant usually just fades into the mulch. But if it doesn't, just cut it back to the crown with fall or winter cleanup.

Geranium x *oxianum* '**Claridge Druce**' has escaped notice when grown among *Iris spuria, Iris sibirica, Lychnis coronaria,* or any large ornamental grasses. Or it may be deer-resistant.

Geranium sanguinium lancastriense was eaten by the deer in my garden, perhaps because the plant was not protected by other deer-resistant plants.

Geranium '**Johnson's Blue**' and *Geranium incanum* were loved by the deer!

Geranium robertianum is a very invasive weed.

HELENIUM

Helenium autumnale
(sneezeweed)

Helenium autumnale must be named for their beautiful array of fall colors, attractive to butterflies. One of the strongest herbaceous perennials in the border, sneezeweed is colorful for most of the summer.

DESCRIPTION

Strong, upright growth is medium-green, adding beautiful color and form to the spring and early summer border. By midsummer, 4-foot stalks are branching and beginning to flower. A mature plant has a crown of about 18 inches with as much as a 3- to 4-foot spread in bloom. Named cultivars are available in beautiful warm colors.

CULTURAL REQUIREMENTS

Zones 3–10. *Helenium autumnale* is a good herbaceous perennial for even the coldest zones in the western, northwestern and southwestern United States.

Full sun to very light shade is the best exposure for this plant. Flowering is dependant upon optimal sun exposure.

Sneezeweed performs best in good garden soil with plentiful compost and organic phosphorus added. A 2-inch mulch is very important to conserve moisture.

Regular watering once a week is essential, or *Helenium autumnale* will show signs of stress (dried lower leaves). Grown in drier conditions, *Helenium* will have fewer flowers.

BLOOM

Helenium autumnale

There are so many choices of warm colors with *Helenium!* Rust, red-orange, golden and yellow in solid colors and beautiful shades and blends. Named cultivars are solid colors, but this plant crosses, and the seedlings may have some of the most beautiful markings.

Helenium autumnale begins bloom in midsummer and continues until fall if it is deadheaded, with each flowerhead removed as soon as it fades.

Helenium is an attractive cut flower with a very strong stem. However, cutting the stalk with its sprays of flowers and buds will lessen the color in your border, since each stalk produces blooms over several weeks.

SEASONAL INTEREST

Adding interest to the border as soon as it begins growth at the end of winter, *Helenium* is a strong structural perennial. By mid-summer in most climates, its colorful blooms are showy even from a distance.

Seedheads are interesting, and may be left on the plant toward the end of the summer, when you are certain that there are no more buds to be opened.

COMPANION PLANTS AND LANDSCAPE USE

Helenium is a handsome plant with many other perennials. A cultivar with rust flowers such as 'Mardi Gras' (planted in the Blooms of Bressingham Perennial Evaluation Garden at the Center for Urban Horticulture in Seattle WA) would be striking with the golden flowers of *Rudbeckia fulgida* 'Goldsturm' and the pale-pink of *Penstemon* 'Evelyn'. This rust cultivar is taller than the other two perennials, and it may be placed behind them in the border.

With the golden or yellow *Helenium,* white Shasta daisies (*Leucanthemum x superbum*) or feverfew (*Tanacetum parthenium*) or maiden grass (*Miscanthus sinensis*) are very pleasing.

Caryopteris clandonensis is drought-tolerant, but it will also do well in an irrigated border, and its sky-blue flowers are a perfect complement for any of the warm colors of *Helenium.*

The attractive lower foliage of the *Helenium* allows it to be used toward the front of the border. In my border, there are even taller perennials blooming at the same time (*Solidago, Helianthus maximilianii*) in the same color range. *Helenium* looks like an edging plant grown near these taller perennials!

Montbretia (*Crocosmia crocosmiiflora*) is a wonderful companion with *Helenium autumnale.*

PROPAGATION

Clumps of *Helenium* are easily divided during the dormant season. Colors may not come true from seed, but the crosses may offer some intriguing combinations. Seed germinates easily in warm soil but this plant has not self-sown in my garden.

MAINTENANCE

Deadheading individual flowers is painstaking, but rewards the diligent gardener with an extended bloom season because each cluster of blooms lasts longer.

Maintenance, most often done in fall, consists of cutting the stalks all the way back to the crown. This task may be done as soon as the plant looks spent at the end of its season.

Helianthus angustifolius

Helianthus angustifolius
(swamp sunflower)

Thriving in an irrigated border, *Helianthus angustifolius* is one of two *Helianthus* that have not been eaten by the deer in my garden. The last of the herbaceous perennials to bloom, this *Helianthus* is one of the most glorious of all the perennials!

DESCRIPTION

With rich dark-green foliage, and many slender leaves along the stem, this sunflower has a lush appearance through the spring and summer months. Its growth habit is strongly upright for weeks. As it reaches bloom height, a mature plant is 4 to 5 feet in height, and slightly arching. In bloom, an abundance of yellow daisies open in succession for several weeks. As bloom progresses, the arching habit increases, which means this plant needs at least 4 to 5 feet in width in the border. Each plant at the crown has a spread of 2 to 3 feet.

CULTURAL REQUIREMENTS

Zones 3–10. Full sun is the exposure needed to maximize the bloom of this plant. Because it blooms so late, be attentive to your fall light in the garden. *Helianthus angustifolius* will need to be in full sun in September and October, just before and during bloom.

Garden soil will need to be rich with lots of compost and organic phosphorus, and an added mulch.

For the best-looking plant with the most flowers, irrigate deeply once a week. Despite its name, swamp sunflower does not need to be wet, but should not be allowed to dry out. The leaves look good during the growing season when *Helianthus* is grown in good soil with irrigation.

BLOOM

Beautiful yellow daisies, 2 to 3 inches in diameter, open on very slender stems off the primary sturdy stalk in early fall. Each stalk of *Helianthus angustifolius* holds so many flowers that a single plant is an incredible sight in fall. This is truly one of the most beautiful perennials, and what a gift at the end of the season!

Individual flower stems are seldom long enough for taller bouquets, but *Helianthus angustifolius* is an excellent cut flower if you're willing to cut most of the stalk.

If you have given *Helianthus angustifolius* enough room in your border, allow the arching stems to be natural and do not stake them. This cascading habit is part of the beauty of this plant in my garden.

In climates where your late summer to fall season is cut short by cold temperatures, the gardener should definitely deadhead individual flowers as they bloom so that the plant puts energy into more bloom.

COMPANION PLANTS AND LANDSCAPE USE

Late-blooming bluebeard (*Caryopteris incana*) is the perfect companion, with its rich, blue flowers complementary to the yellow sunflower. Similarly, plumabago (*Ceratostigma willmottianum*), with its late blue flowers and fall red foliage makes a dynamic companion.

As ornamental grasses turn to gold and rust in fall, they are beautiful companions. *Helianthus angustifolius* growing near maiden grass (*Miscanthus sinensis*) or blue stem (*Schizachyrium scoparium*) is a wonderful combination. Remember to give each plant the space it needs for best performance.

All of the companions mentioned create a beautiful fall scene near the paperbark maple (*Acer griseum*). *Helianthus angustifolius* is a perfect addition for a dynamic fall focal spot in the waning garden.

Because this sunflower has such a rich, green foliage, upright growth habit, and perfect form, it is a wonderful addition to an herbaceous border. It looks good the entire growing season.

PROPAGATION

Helianthus angustifolius roots very quickly from vegetative cuttings taken before the plant blooms.

MAINTENANCE

Deadheading will prolong bloom. This is especially important to do if you live in a cold climate. In our Indian summer in the Sierra foothills, the bloom of *Helianthus angustifolius* is several weeks long, even when it is not deadheaded.

Fall or winter maintenance consists of cutting the stalks back to the crown, and renewing the mulch.

Helianthus maximilianii
(native perennial sunflower)

One of my favorite gardening friends, Harry Stowe, when he was in his late eighties, drove into my driveway unexpectedly one spring day, a box of roots with slightly wilting stalks in the back of his truck. He presented them simply: "You don't have this in your garden, and I think you should!" And he was off, back to his own garden some 15 miles away. No bits of cultural advice, no warnings, and no comments about deer. In bloom, this tall, robust sunflower always reminds me of Harry.

DESCRIPTION

Native to central and southwestern United States, *Helianthus maximilianii* is the tallest herbaceous perennial in my garden. Definitely not suitable for the small garden, this perennial sunflower reaches heights of 5 to 6 feet. With a strong spreading habit, this plant can take up a lot of room in the garden. The beautiful gray-green leaves are 8 to 10 inches long.

CULTURAL REQUIREMENTS

Zones 3–10. It will grow in the coldest regions of the western, southwestern and northwestern United States. Full sun to very light shade is the best exposure, as it is for all of the sunflowers.

In fertile garden soil, with lots of compost added, the height of *Helianthus maximilianii* will be quite tall. In poorer soils, the height will be reduced, but the plant may look stressed in summer heat. Try a compromise of some compost and phosphorus, and a good organic mulch, but don't make your soil too rich. One-third compost to two-thirds native soil is the best ratio.

Irrigation once a week is required for good performance of this perennial sunflower in my hot climate. In cooler climates, with a good mulch, this native sunflower is more drought-tolerant.

BLOOM

Multiple yellow daisies 3 to 4 inches in diameter open along the tall flowering stalks. Bloom begins in midsummer and may continue for several weeks. Individual flowers are on very short stems off the main stalk.

This is a good cut flower, but the entire flower stalk would need to be cut when it is in its prime.

Deadheading is not necessary, but may extend the bloom, especially in a short-season climate.

SEASONAL INTEREST

Helianthus maximilianii is a very handsome plant with strong growth in early spring. For several weeks, beautiful stalks of rich gray-green leaves add color, textural interest, form, and increasing height to my herbaceous border. Bloom is the finale.

COMPANION PLANTS AND LANDSCAPE USE

My favorite companion is feverfew *(Tanacetum parthenium)* which has self-sown within the planting of *Helianthus maximilianii*. Clearly, the feverfew does not mind root competition. Its delicate foliage and white flowers come up through the bold gray-green foliage of the sunflower. In my garden, there seems to be no other companion so perfectly matched with *Helianthus maximilianii*.

If plenty of room is allowed for the sunflower roots, other tall herbaceous perennials may be used nearby such as goldenrod *(Solidago)* or sneezeweed *(Helenium autumnale)*, both of which bloom about the same time. Another sunflower, *Helianthus angustifolius* is a nice companion with contrasting foliage color. It will bloom after the *Helianthus maximilianii*.

The taller barberries *(Berberis atropurpurea, B. darwinii)* are strong companions. *Helianthus maximilianii* could also be planted near Oregon grape holly *(Mahonia aquifolium)*, Artemisia 'Powis Castle', or silverberry *(Elaeagnus pungens)*. All of the companions mentioned provide good contrast in leaf color and form, and plant form and structure.

Maiden grass *(Miscanthus sinensis)* is an excellent companion.

PROPAGATION

Helianthus maximilianii is easily divided during the dormant season. Vegetative cuttings may also be taken prior to bud formation.

MAINTENANCE

Cut stalks back to the crown when they are no longer attractive, or during your fall or winter cleanup. Keep this plant mulched with 2 to 3 inches of organic material.

Lift roots at the edge of the clump at any time to control invasiveness.

Helianthus multiflorus **'Lodden Gold'** and **'Summer Sun'** have been eaten by the deer in my garden.

Helleborus argutifolius

HELLEBORUS

Three hellebores have been tested for deer-resistance in my garden, and in other gardens with a deer population. These have been left alone consistently, so it is likely that other species within this genus are also deer-resistant. All are wonderful evergreen perennials, especially to add winter interest to the shade or semi-shade garden.

Helleborus argutifolius, H. corsicus
(Corsican hellebore)

Helleborus argutifolius is a very distinctive evergreen perennial.

DESCRIPTION

Helleborus argutifolius is 3 feet tall, and a mature plant is as wide. Handsome leaves are large and long-lived, light blue-green and sharply-toothed along the edges. Plants may not bloom the first year after planting.

CULTURAL REQUIREMENTS

Zones 6–10. This is a strong perennial that does not do well in the coldest regions of the west (below 10°F in winter), but is also the only hellebore that will perform in the warm winters of southern California. It is the most tolerant of sun and does not seem to like deep shade. In my garden in the hot Sierra foothills, *Helleborus argutifolius* has done very well in semi-shade.

In cooler coastal climates, Corsican hellebore may be grown in full sun. *Helleborus argutifolius* will not need as much irrigation where summer temperatures stay below 85°F, as long as it is mulched.

Prepare soil with lots of compost and organic phosphorus. This perennial will not be disturbed for years. Add a layer of mulch of at least 2 inches, renewing it each spring before seeds mature.

Irrigation should be deep (to 12 inches), and as frequent as every 1 to 2 weeks.

BLOOM

When the plant has had a chance to settle in for a year, the following spring very strong flower stalks have as many as twenty nodding, apple-green, cup-shaped flowers. Flowers hold their form and color for 2 months or more, beginning in early spring. Even as they fade, the developing seedpods are interesting.

Corsican hellebore is an excellent cut flower. Stems must be conditioned as bulbs are: sear the cut end with a flame, or very hot water, then place into cold water.

SEASONAL INTEREST

Helleborus argutifolius is a perfect perennial for year-round interest in a large or small garden. An evergreen with very attractive leaves, the flowers are an added bonus and very long-lasting.

Snows rarely damage Corsican hellebore because the stems for both leaf and flowers are so strong.

COMPANION PLANTS AND LANDSCAPE USE

An evergreen groundcover, *Lamium maculatum* is a perfect companion for year-round interest. Corsican hellebore is also very beautiful with sweet woodruff (*Galium odoratum*), its dainty leaves and flowers a delicate contrast with the strong form of the *Helleborus argutifolius*.

The Corsican hellebore is excellent in a container, and can be placed in full sun in any climate in the winter. Move the container into partial shade in late spring and summer so there will be no stress to the plant.

All the hellebores are beautiful planted with *Rhododendron* species and Mexican orange (*Choisya ternata*).

Variegated ornamental grasses recommended for lady's mantle (*Alchemilla mollis*) are wonderful companions for *Helleborus argutifolius*.

PROPAGATION

All the hellebores self-sow easily, but plants are slow to develop. Be careful to spread compost in the fall so that seeds of the early bloomers can nestle into the mulch. If you are allowing hellebores to self-sow, you do not want to cover the seed after it has dropped. Leaves falling from deciduous trees must be removed from the seedbed. Seed will be stratified during the winter, and germinate the following spring. Nature knows best!

Leave the seedlings in place, or lift carefully in late spring and grow them where they will have no competition for light, nutrients, or moisture. Tiny seedlings mature slowly (3 years or more).

MAINTENANCE

Remove spent flower stalks after seeds have dropped or been gathered. Cut the stalk to the crown of the plant. Spent leaves are few, but may be removed at any time during the growing season.

Helleborus foetidus
(stinky hellebore)

Helleborus foetidus

An unfortunate common name, but it suggests that a gardener did not like the smell when the leaves were crushed. Don't crush the tropical-looking leaves, and this evergreen perennial will be a welcome addition in your shade garden.

DESCRIPTION

Helleborus foetidus has a tropical look, with several 8- to 10-inch, slim, dark-green leaflets arranged in a fan. The height is slightly shorter than Helleborus argutifolius, 2 to 3 feet.

CULTURAL REQUIREMENTS

Zones 3–10. *Helleborus foetidus* will grow in the coldest regions of the western, southwestern, and northwestern United States.

Partial shade is the best exposure. Too much sun will burn the leaves, and deep or total shade will lessen flowering.

Soil requirements are the same as for *Helleborus argutifolius*. But this hellebore requires more water, with deep irrigation once a week.

BLOOM

The green cup-shaped flowers are very similar to the Corsican hellebore, but each flower is edged with red, a very subtle marking that adds to its attractiveness. Cut flowers must be treated as for *Helleborus argutifolius*.

SEASONAL INTEREST

Same as for *Helleborus argutifolius*.

COMPANION PLANTS AND LANDSCAPE USE

Same as for *Helleborus argutifolius*. A lovely container plant.

PROPAGATION

Same as for *Helleborus argutifolius*.

MAINTENANCE

Same as for *Helleborus argutifolius*.

Helleborus orientalis
(Lenten rose)

Helleborus orientalis

The first of the late-winter perennials to bloom, along with violets, evergreen Lenten rose is a delight! There are several hybrid cultivars.

DESCRIPTION

Helleborus orientalis is shorter than the other two species of *Helleborus* described. Its leaflets are in fans like *Helleborus foetidus*, but each leaflet is broader and there are fewer leaflets to a fan. Leaves are a rich dark-green and shiny. The plant is 18 to 24 inches in height and spread.

CULTURAL REQUIREMENTS

Zones 3–10. This hellebore will grow in the coldest regions of the west, southwest, and northwest. It is best in semi-shade and will also tolerate deep shade.

Soil preparation and irrigation are the same as for *Helleborus argutifolius*.

BLOOM

The flowers are quite different from the other two hellebores described. Individual flowers of the species *Helleborus orientalis* are open, with exquisite dark markings on the light-green to creamy-green petals. Flowers nod slightly, a characteristic of this genus, and are borne in a cluster at the end of a strong 1-foot stem.

Flowers of the hybrids vary in shades of rose, some with very attractive deep colors.

Cut flowers must be treated as for *Helleborus argutifolius*.

SEASONAL INTEREST

Same as for *Helleborus argutifolius*.

COMPANION PLANTS AND LANDSCAPE USE

Same as for *Helleborus argutifolius*.

PROPAGATION

Same as for *Helleborus argutifolius*.

MAINTENANCE

At the end of a cold winter, *Helleborus orientalis* tends to have a few shabby-looking leaves that should be removed by cutting the leaf stems at the crown. The new leaves will quickly follow in spring.

IRIS

With several hundred cultivars to choose from, gardeners must select *Iris* for their adaptability to a given microclimate as they would with any perennial. *Iris* are noted for their deer-resistance. This selection is limited to three that have been excellent performers in my garden: *Iris sibirica* and *Iris spuria* which are both herbaceous and known since the 16th century, and *Iris unguicularis,* an evergreen relatively unknown in gardens today, but first noted in 1865 in Europe.

Iris sibirica
(Siberian iris)

Variable from dwarf to tall cultivars, herbaceous Siberian iris has an interesting range of colors and form. Be certain that your selection is accurately labeled when you purchase from a grower or nursery.

DESCRIPTION

Dwarf cultivars may be a foot or less in height, while the taller cultivars are 3 to 4 feet. Colors vary from beautiful white, through a range of blue and violet. Some Siberian iris have very upright growth habit and some more loose. Arching leaves are long and slender, a beautiful dark-green.

CULTURAL REQUIREMENTS

Zones 2–10. This herbaceous iris does well in the coldest regions of the western, southwestern, and northwestern United States. Full sun to very light shade is required for optimal flowering and plant vigor.

Iris sibirica needs to grow in good soil with plenty of compost and organic phosphorus added, and a mulch.

Irrigation should be deep and regular, at least once a week in hot climates during the summer. Unlike many iris, this species is not drought-tolerant.

BLOOM

Iris sibirica is a beardless iris. Colors include white, shades of blue and violet, pink, and a light-yellow. Some have very beautiful markings. One of the most beautiful flowers for late-spring and early-summer display, Siberian iris are also very attractive in bud. Flowers do not last long, especially in warm weather, but they are very striking while in bloom.

This is excellent cut flower. Stems are very strong and quite long, except on the dwarf cultivars.

Do not deadhead mature plants if you have allowed the plants to flower without gathering bouquets. Very attractive seedpods will follow the fleeting blossoms. Siberian iris is an excellent everlasting, holding its form and dark brown color for years.

SEASONAL INTEREST

Iris sibirica is very attractive with its early spring growth of slender leaves. This is one of the best of the herbaceous perennials for form and texture in the border.

While the bloom is short, seedpods are an added attraction by mid-summer. Seedpods are at first green, then change to brown as fall approaches. No need to gather this everlasting until the first snowfall.

COMPANION PLANTS AND LANDSCAPE USE

Iris sibirica offers wonderful contrast because of its leaf form. Plan to use it as a single specimen, or a drift of several plants in your irrigated border. Its strength of foliage will become a focal point in spring and early summer.

Grow Santa Barbara daisy *(Erigeron karvinskianus)* at the base of Siberian iris. *Buphthalmum* is another worthy companion.

Rudbeckia fulgida 'Goldsturm' foliage is a beautiful contrast of leaf and plant form, and blooms after the Siberian iris. As fall approaches, these two plants have contrasting seedheads that are dynamic additions to the late border.

Any perennial requiring the same exposure, soil, and moisture, combines beautifully with Siberian iris, as long as the two are compatible in height. Taller perennials should not be allowed to overshadow this beautiful plant.

A single specimen of *Iris sibirica* may be used in a large border or in the small garden. Siberian iris is also excellent in containers.

PROPAGATION

Divisions of *Iris sibirica* are easily made during the dormant season. Lift established clumps and cut them apart, or cut into the crown, removing a portion to be divided.

MAINTENANCE

If plants look spent from summer heat, they may be cut back to the crown. This will stimulate new growth, although it may not be as tall as the first growth of the season.

During fall or winter cleanup, cut all growth back to the crown and renew the mulch.

Division of older clumps may be necessary to reinvigorate a plant that has been in the garden for several years.

Iris spuria

Found in old country gardens, long abandoned by the original gardener, *Iris spuria* continues to grow and bloom, year after year, with no attention. Clumps are very handsome and will die back only when the summer months are very dry.

DESCRIPTION

Even in tough conditions, this herbaceous perennial is 3 to 4 feet tall. Its bold, dark-green foliage shows dynamic strength in spring, and with sufficient moisture, may reach a height of 5 feet. Clumps spread slowly.

CULTURAL REQUIREMENTS

Zones 5–9. This herbaceous iris does well in the coldest regions of the western, southwestern, and northwestern United States. It grows well in considerable shade, but needs more sunlight for bloom. Full sun to light shade is recommended for *Iris spuria*.

Good garden soil is not necessary for this rugged perennial. However, in my herbaceous border where the soil has been amended with compost, the clump of *Iris spuria* is thriving and the foliage lasts longer through the hot summer months.

Irrigation is not needed for good flowering or spring foliage growth. However, summer irrigation will prolong the foliage display into fall.

BLOOM

In old gardens you will find white or yellow, or a combination of the two colors. A broader color range is available with the hybrids. Flowering is short, in early summer.

SEASONAL INTEREST

Iris spuria

Iris spuria has very handsome foliage for many weeks. In the hot dry garden, the foliage will fade when there has been no rain for a month. Gardeners in cool and warm climates may consider this plant drought-tolerant.

With irrigation or rains during the summer, this striking perennial is a strong addition to the border.

COMPANION PLANTS AND LANDSCAPE USE

In the dry garden, *Achillea filipendulina* 'Coronation Gold', *Artemisia* 'Powis Castle', or *Achillea* x 'Moonshine' are great companions for *Iris spuria*. The foliage and form are lovely in contrast. Matilija poppy *(Romneya coulteri)* also has beautifully contrasting foliage color, and its flowers echo the colors of yellow and white in the *Iris spuria*.

Caryopteris clandonensis will bloom later, but its delicate gray-green foliage is nice with the dark-green of the iris. In a drier garden, the

Caryopteris planted in front of the iris will take over as the focal spot when the iris begins to fade.

The handsome dark-green foliage adds interest to any herbaceous border. This plant is tall, and should be placed near other tall perennials such as goldenrod *(Solidago)*, or perennial sunflower *(Helianthus maximilianii)*. Plant black-eyed Susan *(Rudbeckia fulgida* 'Goldsturm') in front of *Iris spuria*.

PROPAGATION

Make divisions from established clumps during the dormant season. *Iris spuria* can be very difficult to divide, and it may be necessary to use a sharp tool, cutting through the fleshy roots.

MAINTENANCE

Cut faded foliage back to the crown when it looks shabby or after it has died back.

Iris unguicularis
(winter iris)

Winter iris is an evergreen that begins bloom in mid-December in my garden, with iris blossoms nestled in the dark-green foliage. The strongest perennial for bloom during the dormant season, *Iris unguicularis* blooms heedless of temperatures to 10°F, and occasional snowfalls.

DESCRIPTION

Winter iris has very narrow dark-green leaves with a graceful arching and mounding habit. Flowers show just above the foliage. An established clump can be as broad as 2 to 3 feet. Height is under 18 inches. *Iris unguicularis* is a very handsome evergreen iris for all seasons.

CULTURAL REQUIREMENTS

Zones 8–10. Winter iris will not survive in the coldest regions, but is very winter-hardy to 10°F, and still looks good when 3 feet of snow melts.

Winter iris is a tough plant that does not need rich soil. However, the addition of compost and organic phosphorus will increase the blooming and strength of *Iris unguicularis.*

Iris unguicularis is very tolerant of dry shade, and also does well in full sun with summer irrigation every 2 weeks. Gardeners in the hottest summer climates should plant this winter iris where it is shaded from the afternoon sun. A few hours of sunlight or strong light in winter will be necessary for bloom.

Winter iris does not need to be irrigated during the dry summer months in those climates that have little or no rain from June through September. It will tolerate irrigation and wet clay soils in winter if there is good drainage.

In competition with root systems of nearby ornamental shrubs or trees, *Iris unguicularis* still performs well.

BLOOM

Fragrant flowers are often somewhat hidden by foliage, but their colors are a clear contrast to the dark-green, and they always show through with shades of light and dark lavender, orchid pink, or white.

The bloom of *Iris unguicularis* extends through the winter months from as early as November, through March.

No deadheading is needed, but since there are few other garden tasks when this plant is in bloom, removing faded flowers will allow the plant to put energy into more blooming, and bring the gardener outside to enjoy the fragrance.

SEASONAL INTEREST

A winter bloomer that is evergreen and a modest size, *Iris unguicularis* must be one of the best perennial for any garden! Winter iris always looks good in my garden where it is in a spot of dry shade near the porch, brightening my winter days.

COMPANION PLANTS AND LANDSCAPE USE

Long, slender iris foliage is a pleasing contrast with the leaves of Mexican orange, (*Choisya ternata*) or *Daphne odora*, two ornamental shrubs with similar requirements. Violets (*Viola odorata*) are an attractive groundcover, completing this winter focal area. Since each one of these plants is fragrant, it is fortunate that they do not all open their flowers at once.

Sweet vanilla plant (*Sarcococca ruscifolia*) is another fragrant winter-blooming ornamental shrub in my dry shade garden that is a good companion to winter iris. Their dark-green leaves are similar in color but very contrasting in form.

Tiny blue *Scilla* and white *Galanthus* are bulbs to plant near the winter iris.

Use winter iris in the woodland garden. Planted in drifts of several large clumps, *Iris unguicularis* will add interest in all seasons.

A single clump of winter iris in a small garden or in a container is effective.

PROPAGATION

Winter iris is propagated by making divisions in late winter after bloom. A clump may be divided at any time during the spring. Blooming may be disrupted if divisions are made in late summer or in fall.

MAINTENANCE

EASY! No maintenance is needed except for the occasional removal of old leaves. My winter iris has not been groomed for at least two years, and still looks great.

LAVANDULA

English lavenders and the closely related lavandins are ideal subshrubs for the dry garden. My first brush with lavender was in Santa Rosa, California, where one of my great aunts had a cottage garden between her Victorian house and the carriage house. The lavender was one of the few plants to survive when I visited again, 20 years later. But then again, perhaps it was not the same lavender. However, for me, it was the most important memory of her wonderful garden.

DESCRIPTION

Lavandula angustifolia

Height and spread of this subshrub are when the plant is not in bloom. Flowering stems will add 12 to 18 inches to the height and often to the spread. The flower stalks of lavandins tend to be more upright, and usually add only 1 foot to the spread in bloom. The length of the flower stem varies depending on the cultivar, and how the plant is grown (soil, irrigation, exposure).

Shades of gray foliage vary for each cultivar, with the English lavenders having grayer foliage, sometimes with a blue or green cast, and the lavandins having gray-white foliage.

Root systems are large and resent disturbance. Moving an established plant from one spot in garden to another is rarely successful.

Because there are so many different cultivars, and each one has different characteristics, the ones grown in my garden are listed here:

THE FRAGRANT LAVENDERS

Lavandula angustifolia (English lavender): the species, 3-foot height and spread, light-lavender flowers.

Lavandula angustifolia 'Alba' (English lavender): 3-foot height and spread, white flowers.

Lavandula angustifolia 'Blue Cushion' (English lavender): very compact, 1-foot height and spread, light-lavender flowers.

Lavandula angustifolia 'Hidcote' (English lavender): 18-inch height and spread, dark-lavender flowers.

Lavandula angustifolia 'Alba'

Lavandula angustifolia 'Hidcote Giant' (English lavender): 2 to 3-foot height and spread, dark-lavender flowers.

Lavandula angustifolia 'Jean Davis' (English lavender): small and compact, 12- to 15-inch height and spread, pale-pink flowers, short display of color.

Lavandula angustifolia 'Munstead' (English lavender): open growth habit, 2-foot height, 3-foot spread, dark-purple flowers, longest bloom of all lavenders tested, somewhat untidy.

Lavandula angustifolia 'Vera' (English lavender): very compact growth habit, 18-inch height and spread, dark-purple flowers, long bloom, perfect for "hedges" or edging.

Lavandula angustifolia nana 'Alba' (English lavender): low (under 1-foot height) and wide (3-foot spread), short flower stems with white flowers, long-lasting color display.

THE FRAGRANT LAVANDINS

Lavandula x *intermedia* 'Dutch': 2-foot height and spread, very dense, medium-length flower stems, light-lavender flowers.

Lavandula x *intermedia* 'Dutch Mill': 3-foot height and spread, very dense, medium-length flower stems, light-lavender flowers.

Lavandula x *intermedia* 'Fred Boutin': huge! 3- to 4-foot height and up to 5-foot spread, flowering stems to 12 to 15 inches above this height, light-lavender flowers, long-lasting display.

Lavandula x *intermedia* '**Grosso**': very compact plant, 18-inch height and spread, long upright flower stems to 2 feet, light-lavender flowers.

Lavandula x *intermedia* '**Provence**': 2- to 3-foot height and spread, medium length flower stems, light-lavender flowers.

Lavandula x *intermedia* '**White Spike**': 2- to 3-foot height and spread, long flower stems to 18 inches, white flowers.

CULTURAL REQUIREMENTS

Zones 5–8. Full sun is very important for all the lavenders and lavandins. Any shade, including that from another plant growing too close, will affect growth habit and bloom.

Soil should be lean: not too much compost, but still be generous with organic phosphorus. Do not mulch with compost. One of the best mulches for lavender is gravel!

If you garden where the climate and soils are described as "Mediterranean", lighten the clay soil with very aged compost. Winter drainage is especially important.

Hot exposures are the best. In a cooler climate, plant *Lavandula* in a southern exposure where it will get reflected heat from a wall, building, sidewalk, or driveway. Rocks nearby will also create a warmer microclimate.

When lavenders and lavandins are mature, they are drought-tolerant. Plant them in dry gardens or gardens of very little irrigation (once every 3 weeks in the heat of the summer where temperatures are above 90 degrees).

BLOOM

See descriptions for each cultivar above. All are very fragrant and may be used for fresh cut flowers. If you are drying *Lavandula,* cut stems when the flowers are first opening, and spread the stalks in a shady place.

Length of flower stem depends on how it is grown. Increased irrigation or soil fertility may lengthen the flower stalks, but it may also shorten the life of the plant.

Length of bloom depends, as with most perennials, on summer heat. Gardeners in cooler climates, where summer temperatures rarely rise above 85°F, may enjoy lavender in bloom all summer into fall.

SEASONAL INTEREST

Lavandula looks good all year as long as its cultural and maintenance requirements have been met. It blooms for several weeks, beginning in early summer.

COMPANION PLANTS AND LANDSCAPE USE

Lavandula angustifolia 'Vera'

With attention to the eventual size, *Lavandula* may be used with any other low-irrigation plant. *Coreopsis* has several cultivars with varying sizes from low to tall. *Coreopsis verticillata* 'Moonbeam' is attractive with the low *Lavandula angustifolia nana* 'Alba'. *Coreopsis lanceolata* combines beautifully with the larger *Lavandula*, and *Coreopsis grandiflora* would be a compatible size with the very large *Lavandula* 'Fred Boutin'.

Lavenders and lavandins are excellent in the rock garden, where trailing and creeping perennials offer contrasting color of bloom and foliage. Some of the favorites in my rock garden include snow-in-summer (*Cerastium tomentosum*), thymes (*Thymus*), creeping baby's breath (*Gypsophila repens*), and creeping germanders (*Teucrium cossonii majoricum* and *Teucrium* x *lucidrys* 'Prostratum').

Rosemary (*Rosmarinus officinalis*) in its upright form is a strong structural plant to pair with the larger lavenders and lavandins. Upright germander (*Teucrium* x *lucidrys*, *T. chamaedrys*) is also strong in structure, but smaller than most of the lavenders. Germander begins blooming as the lavender wanes in my hot-summer climate, and its rich, dark-green leaves are year-round contrast. All three of these perennials planted near each other are excellent evergreen and evergray combinations for the winter garden.

Anthemis tinctoria is a beautiful companion with the midsized and larger *Lavandula*.

Caryopteris clandonensis is a good companion, beginning bloom as the lavender fades. The gray-green leaves of the *Caryopteris* are very attractive as a contrast with the silvers and grays of *Lavandula*.

If you are using *Lavandula* as a hedge along a walkway, allow for the eventual spread of the plant in bloom. If the plant must be pruned when it is in bloom so that people can walk by it, you will lose the beauty of form. Edging plants such as *Thymus* and *Teucrium* x *lucidrys* 'Prostratum' may be used between the lavenders, or the lavender and the walkway, to fill the space. The green cultivars of thyme and germander will tolerate any shade that might be cast by its neighboring lavender.

PROPAGATION

Lavandula cannot be divided. Vegetative cuttings should be taken after bloom, midsummer into fall. Cuttings root easily in a medium of one-half vermiculite and one-half perlite, when they are in a hothouse. Place your trays on a gravel bed to allow young roots to develop in a medium that drains quickly. Cuttings should be ready for potting up in 8 weeks. Late cuttings may be held inside a hothouse or cold frame through the winter.

MAINTENANCE

Lavandula may be pruned with hedge clippers right after bloom. This will remove a portion of the new growth, but the plant will quickly branch with more new shoots, and occasionally rebloom. This method of pruning encourages thick growth and a more attractive plant.

Harvesting *Lavandula* should be done when flowers first open and the fragrance is strongest. One year *Lavandula* 'Grosso' was harvested for my great-aunt's retirement community, and it rebloomed heavily a few weeks later.

If you prefer to leave the fading flowers on *Lavandula* for the textural effect, your pruning may be done in late winter.

Pruning to old wood is not recommended, but may be done on healthy, vigorous plants. It may take two years or more for the plant to recover with new growth.

Lavandula stoechas
(Spanish lavender)

Spanish lavender is a more tender woody subshrub (zones 5–9) that may be damaged in severe winter cold below 10°F. *Lavandula stoechas* is 2 to 3 feet in height and spread. Spanish lavender is more open in its growth habit. Its deep-purple flowers have often been described as butterflies. The flowers are not fragrant, but are attractive to bees and butterflies. Cultural requirements and landscape use are the same as for other *Lavandula*. There is a dwarf variety with white flowers but it is not as attractive as the whites of *Lavandula angustifolia* or *Lavandula* x *intermedia*.

A Pacific Northwest gardener reports that this lavender has been a better performer than the English lavenders or lavandins in his garden. It has tolerated some shade and more cold.

Lavandula dentata
(French lavender)

French lavender is also deer-resistant, but usually hardy only where winter temperatures stay above 20° F. *Lavandula dentata* gets very large, 3 to 4 feet in height and spread. Cultural requirements are the same as for other *Lavandula*. Flowers are light-lavender. Because of its size, use larger drought-tolerant perennials such as Matilija poppy (*Romneya coulteri*) and upright rosemary (*Rosmarinus officinalis*) as companions.

In very warm microclimates in the Pacific Northwest, this lavender is winter-hardy.

Leucanthemum x *superbum*

LEUCANTHEMUM

Leucanthemum x *superbum*
(Shasta daisy)

Previously classified as a *Chrysanthemum,* Shasta daisy has been known in gardens since the early 19th century. Shasta daisies offer a range of heights. A showy perennial, *Leucanthemum* x *superbum* (also classified as *Leucanthemum maximum*) belongs in every garden, from the smallest garden room to the largest country estate!

DESCRIPTION

Shasta daisies spread strongly, but not aggressively. Very dark-green leathery leaves, 4 to 6 inches or more in length, are attractive when the plant is not blooming. Dwarf cultivars bloom under 2 feet in height, and the tallest may be as much as 4 feet. Foliage may be evergreen in the warmest climates, but this daisy is usually considered herbaceous.

CULTURAL REQUIREMENTS

Zones 3–10. Shasta daisies do well in the coldest zones of the western, southwestern, and northwestern United States. This robust perennial thrives in full sun or part shade. Dappled sunlight under deciduous trees also works as an exposure for Shasta daisies. Gardeners in hot-summer areas should provide some afternoon shade to prolong bloom.

Leucanthemum x *superbum* prefers a good soil, well-augmented with compost and organic phosphorus. Organic mulches should be used to conserve moisture.

Irrigating once every one to two weeks is ideal when plants are mulched. Shasta daisies grown in part shade will not need as much irrigation, as long as they are not in competition with tree roots for available moisture. The leaves of Shasta daisies will wilt on a hot summer day, but will perk up as soon as temperatures cool. *Leucanthemum* x *superbum* is often seen in country gardens, having survived with no irrigation, even in hot climates. Avoid overhead watering of the taller cultivars.

BLOOM

The flowers of all the Shasta daisies are a beautiful white with yellow centers. The dwarf cultivars have somewhat smaller flowers than the larger cultivars. Bloom lasts for several weeks, from early summer to late summer in milder climates.

Listed here are a few that have been grown in my garden:

'Little Miss Muffet' is the smallest cultivar in my garden, with white daisies to 1½ inches in diameter, on 6-inch stalks.

'Snow Lady' is a slightly taller dwarf Shasta daisy, 12 to 15 inches in height in bloom, with a longer bloom period.

'Silver Princess' is my favorite, with strong 18- to 24-inch stalks and a long bloom. This cultivar does not need staking. Flowers are 2 to 3 inches in diameter.

'**Aglaya**' and '**Marconi**' are well-known taller (3 to 4 feet) cultivars that may bloom for weeks if faded flowers are removed. They may need staking, especially in areas where a summer rain is predictable. Flowers are 3 inches or more.

'**Esther Read**' is a long-blooming double white, 3 to 4 feet tall.

SEASONAL INTEREST

Leucanthemum x *superbum*

In the early spring border, the dark-green foliage of *Leucanthemum* x *superbum* is very attractive, but is usually under 1 foot in height, so it may be hidden by taller perennials. The dwarf cultivars are a good addition to the front of the border, since the foliage may be viewed, and the flower stalks are short. In mild climates, the foliage is evergreen. The bloom period is very showy, and when faded flower stalks have been cut back, more leaves will grow for the fall.

COMPANION PLANTS AND LANDSCAPE USE

Be attentive to heights, and use Shasta daisies freely in your borders. The white accent they add is perfect with the warm summer colors of red, orange, gold, and yellow. And with the blues, purples, and pinks, a bright effect is achieved with the addition of Shasta daisies.

The dwarf Shastas are good container plants, and perfect in very small gardens. They are also good edging plants for the larger herbaceous border.

If you are passionate about daisies, plant *Rudbeckia fulgida* 'Goldsturm' with *Leucanthemum* 'Silver Princess'!

PROPAGATION

Shasta daisies are easily divided during the dormant season. They also grow easily from seed sown in the spring when the soil has just begun to warm. Divisions will not need as much attention as young seedlings, and will establish more quickly.

MAINTENANCE

Cut back flowering stalks to the crown when flowers have faded. New growth is attractive in the fall landscape. Renew organic mulch during the dormant season when little growth shows. Very old clumps may need to be divided to invigorate growth.

Leucanthemum vulgare (oxeye daisy) is a white daisy that may look beautiful in a meadow, but is considered a noxious weed in some areas.

LIATRIS

Liatris
(gayfeather, blazing star)

Gayfeather is native to the central and eastern United States. As a garden plant in deer country, it is an outstanding herbaceous perennial for many climates. With interesting foliage and showy flowers, *Liatris* offers a long season of interest.

DESCRIPTION

From tuberous roots, long grassy leaves form tufts of foliage, very attractive in the early spring border. Vertical flower stalks covered with narrow, drooping foliage grow through the late spring and into early summer. Heights vary from the dwarf gayfeather of 2 feet, *Liatris spicata* 'Kobold', to the very tall and more spindly *Liatris pycnostachya* at 6 feet (which might need staking). For most gardens, *Liatris aspera* cultivars with strong stems at 4 to 5 feet will be the best horticultural choices for a taller perennial, and *Liatris spicata* 'Kobold' ('Kobald') for a smaller accent. Height will always depend on soil fertility and available moisture, as with most perennials.

CULTURAL REQUIREMENTS

Zones 3–10. *Liatris* is a wonderful choice for the coldest zones in the western, southwestern, and northwestern United States.

Full sun to light shade is the best exposure, although reflected light from a nearby rock, walk, or building may allow the gardener to place this plant where it gets more shade.

In cultivated gardens, *Liatris* will respond to the addition of organic phosphorus and compost with attractive growth and strength of flower stalks. A good organic mulch is equally important.

As a native wildflower, summer rains will provide the needed moisture where *Liatris* has naturalized. Along the coasts where summers are cool, *Liatris* is definitely drought-tolerant. In hot-summer areas, gayfeather prefers some afternoon shade and irrigation every two weeks, although it will tolerate more frequent watering.

BLOOM

Liatris aspera 'Floristan Violet'

Very showy flowering stalks begin bloom at the top, which is unusual. Color (red-purple or white) lasts for several weeks as fluffy blossoms and the bracts surrounding them continue to show. Bloom begins in midsummer in most climates, and may last into late summer.

Gayfeather is an excellent long-lasting cut flower or dry flower. It attracts beautiful butterflies.

The tallest cultivars may need staking.

SEASONAL INTEREST

Very attractive mid-green foliage adds texture and color to the spring border. As flowering stalks elongate, this grassy texture increases with its height, a wonderful form in the herbaceous border. A large planting of *Liatris aspera* is breathtaking.

Since flowering begins at a time when many other perennials are fading, there's a fresh look to *Liatris* through most of the summer. The rose-purple and even the white flowers are showy color in the garden.

If the vertical interest of fading flower stalks is welcome in your garden, gayfeather will continue to have landscape value into the fall. Fading leafy stalks have a subtle fall color by the end of summer. And if you have remembered to dry a few of the beautiful flowerheads, its memory will linger through winter.

COMPANION PLANTS AND LANDSCAPE USE

Liatris aspera 'Floristan Violet'

Gayfeather is such attractive plant, it is a good addition to any herbaceous border or small garden.

Caryopteris incana and *Ceratostigma species* are beginning to bloom when *Liatris* is colorful. The blue colors reflect the undertones of *Liatris* 'Kobold' growing near it. While the blue mist (*Caryopteris incana*) prefers full sun, in my good garden soil *Liatris* 'Kobold' and *Caryopteris* have done well with sun until four o'clock. A nearby *Ceratostigma willmottianum* shades the *Liatris* first. Remember that plants may create favorable microclimates for each other.

Rudbeckia fulgida 'Goldsturm' is a dynamic companion.

Liatris spicata 'Kobold' and *Coreopsis verticillata* 'Moonbeam' are beautiful companions for each other with contrasting greens and foliage form, and rosy-purple flowers accented against the pale yellow. *Erigeron karvinskianus* is another good companion, the rosy tones in its opening flowerheads an echo of the *Liatris* color.

The dwarf 'Kobold' is an excellent container plant and may be moved into more shade during heat spells, to prolong bloom.

PROPAGATION

Division of the tuberous roots of gayfeather may be easily made when this herbaceous perennial is dormant, or very early in the spring before growth has begun.

MAINTENANCE

Very EASY! Leave plants undisturbed for several years if possible, so that they will establish and increase the number of flowering stalks year after year. When flowers have faded, stalks may be left in place for vertical interest and fall color, or cut back to the crown.

LINARIA

Linaria purpurea
(toadflax)

Linaria purpurea is a delicate perennial in appearance, but so strong in its growth characteristics that many gardeners consider it a weed. Toadflax is a beautiful herbaceous perennial with an airy appearance, that has a place in the large or small garden.

DESCRIPTION

Growth habit of toadflax is strongly vertical, with multiple slender gray-green leaves up to 2 inches in length all along the stalk. Leaves are soft and slightly drooping. Terminal buds have clusters of flowers resembling miniature snapdragons. The overall effect is very wispy, but this plant is strong. Height is dependent on soil fertility. In the best of conditions, *Linaria purpurea* is 3 to 4 feet tall with strong stalks.

CULTURAL REQUIREMENTS

Zones 4–10. *Linaria purpurea* does well in the coldest regions of the western, southwestern, and northwestern United States. Full sun is the best exposure. When grown in shade, toadflax flowers do not have a good strong color, and the plant is weaker.

While it will grow and bloom in the poorest soils, the prettiest plant and the most flowers will result from the addition of organic phosphorus and some good organic compost.

Linaria purpurea is drought-tolerant, but also does well in an irrigated border. If the soil is too moist, lower foliage will turn yellow. Good winter drainage is essential.

BLOOM

Very tiny flowers that look like snapdragons are clustered on the main stalk and side branches, opening first from the bottom. Flowers bloom over a long period of time. The species is purple, and a cultivar 'Canon Went' is pale-pink.

Flowering is strongest in early summer, but if some deadheading is done, *Linaria purpurea* will continue to branch and bloom for most of the summer.

Both the pink and purple toadflax are perfect cut flowers, holding their color for several days, and their form for longer.

SEASONAL INTEREST

Toadflax adds a delicate texture to the spring and summer borders. Sometimes volunteers from a previous year's seeds will germinate as soils warm in the spring, providing fresh new material for the late summer or fall borders.

COMPANION PLANTS AND LANDSCAPE USE

Linaria purpurea is not a showy plant as an individual perennial, but when several are massed together it is a nice effect in the border.

Use *Linaria purpurea* with other sun-loving perennials that have bolder foliage, such as black-eyed Susan (*Rudbeckia fulgida* 'Goldsturm'), purple coneflower (*Echinacea purpurea*), or swamp sunflower (*Helianthus angustifolius*).

The gray-green foliage of *Linaria* is a pleasing counterpoint to the dark-red foliage of barberry *(Berberis thunbergii),* and both are drought-tolerant. Allow the toadflax to weave through the branches of the barberry. Water every 2 to 3 weeks.

PROPAGATION

Linaria is easily propagated from seed sown in the fall or early spring. This perennial will self-sow easily.

MAINTENANCE

Deadhead as needed to extend the bloom season. Seed-saving may be done from one or two flowering heads, gathered when seeds are mature, but before they fall.

Linaria vulgaris is an invasive weed.

LINUM

Linum perenne
(flax)

Linum perenne is the only flax grown in my garden. Because it is often short-lived (five years), this flax is included here for its extraordinary beauty, not its strength as an herbaceous perennial. The flax grown for linen thread is an annual, *Linum usitatissimum.*

DESCRIPTION

Very slender, wiry stems are upright to 2 to 3 feet, with fine slender leaves. Blue flowers open in clusters on side branches and terminal buds, with a slight nodding habit.

CULTURAL REQUIREMENTS

Zones 5–10. While *Linum perenne* may be short-lived, it will grow in the coldest regions of the western, southwestern, and northwestern United States. Heavy wet soils in the winter affect its life span. Full sun and good drainage are necessary.

Linum perenne is a vigorous plant, and not fussy about soil fertility. The addition of organic phosphorus will always ensure a stronger root system and more flowering. Add aged compost to clay or sandy soils. One of the best specimens in my garden was a volunteer in the gravelly edge of my driveway. It thrived there for five years until we had a very cold and wet winter.

This flax is drought-tolerant, and may be adversely affected by overwatering. If you are using it in an herbaceous border that is irrigated, place flax along a dry edge where the sprinkler does not reach. Irrigation every 2 weeks should be adequate.

BLOOM

Linum perenne is strikingly beautiful in bloom. Blue 1-inch flowers open for several weeks beginning in late spring into mid-summer. They open only with sunlight or strong light. Grow this perennial in full sun or with reflected light from a building, wall or fence, especially in areas with lots of cloudy days.

Flax is not a good cut flower because the blooms will close if they are cut.

Flowers will self-sow where soil drains easily. You may need to thin out some of the seedlings to allow only a few plants to mature to their full beauty.

SEASONAL INTEREST

The foliage of *Linum perenne* is very fine. Stems are wiry but flexible, moving with the slightest breeze in the spring. It is the intense blue flowers that become a focal point with a single plant or a drift of several.

As blooms fade, seedpods add an interesting texture to the plant in late summer and fall.

COMPANION PLANTS AND LANDSCAPE USE

Linum perenne has two strengths for the garden: the beautiful blue flowers and the graceful element of movement with wind. Both are fleeting. Place this lovely plant where you will notice it and appreciate its qualities.

Flax begins bloom when the herbaceous border has many perennials blooming. Place it near those requiring the least amount of water: peonies *(Paeonia),* 'Moonshine' yarrow, false indigo *(Baptisia australis),* or *Artemisia* 'Powis Castle'.

PROPAGATION

Linum perenne is easiest from seed. Seedlings are very fine, but stronger than they appear, and may be moved to the desired location. *Linum* self-sows very easily, so there is no need to fuss with special seedling trays or artificial conditions.

MAINTENANCE

Cut back flowering stalks to the crown when flowers have faded. If you are seed-saving or allowing the plant to self-sow, leave seed capsules on the plant until they are mature, then cut back the stalks, scattering the seed on the ground where you want the plants to grow. Do not cover the seed.

LYCHNIS

Lychnis coronaria
(rose campion, rabbit's ears)

Lychnis coronaria is one of my favorite evergray plants. Other names include mullein pink, crown pink, and even dusty miller (which is also a name for several other genuses and species, so this common name can be misleading).

Because rose campion grows easily in a variety of exposures and soil conditions, and because it blooms for so long, this perennial has many uses in my garden. Whether it has naturalized in an old country garden, or was carefully placed by a garden designer, *Lychnis coronaria* seems like a perfect perennial.

DESCRIPTION

The soft white-gray leaves are lance-shaped to 8 inches in length. They form a beautiful evergray rosette under a foot in height, and 12 to 18 inches in spread. From this crown, strong white-gray flowering stalks emerge in spring. The stalks may reach 3 to 4 feet in height and 2 to 3 feet in spread. Magenta, rosy-pink, pale-pink, or white flowers are open and plentiful.

CULTURAL REQUIREMENTS

Lychnis coronaria

Zones 3–10. *Lychnis coronaria* does well in the coldest regions of the western, southwestern, and northwestern United States. Good winter drainage is important. Rose campion does well in either full sun or partial shade. Since competition from nearby roots is not a problem for this hardy perennial, *Lychnis coronaria* is a good choice for the dappled sunlight under deciduous trees.

A little compost and organic phosporus added to the soil is a good idea, but *Lychnis coronaria* does not need a fertile soil. This perennial may not survive rich soils. Strike a balance between fertility and good drainage.

Drought-tolerant, rose campion must have good drainage at all times. An overwatered plant or a plant in wet clay soils in winter will rot and die. *Lychnis coronaria* is excellent choice for the dry garden, including the semi-shade of native oaks. In soils with some compost, it will survive with little or no water.

BLOOM

Attractive round flowers are just under 1 inch in diameter. The species is magenta, an exceptional color in contrast to the gray-white stems and foliage, and the cultivar 'Gardener's World' is a double form of this intense color. The cultivar 'Alba' is white, and there is also a light-pink. Another cultivar, 'Oculata' is white with a bright-pink eye.

Rose campion blooms abundantly in early to midsummer, and even if it is not deadheaded will continue blooming until fall.

Lychnis coronaria is a good cut flower, but because it may bloom for a long time, removing stems for fresh arrangements will reduce the number of flowers in the weeks ahead.

SEASONAL INTEREST

Rose campion is a beautiful light-gray plant even when it is not in bloom, its foliage and form very attractive in the winter garden. In areas of severe winter cold, some leaves may be damaged.

Prolonged bloom adds to the attractiveness of this evergray perennial.

COMPANION PLANTS AND LANDSCAPE USE

As long as the requirement of good drainage is met, *Lychnis coronaria* has multiple uses in the garden. Even in an irrigated herbaceous border, use rose campion along the dry edges.

In dry semi-shade, the white cultivar, 'Alba', brightens the shadows.

Feverfew *(Tanacetum parthenium)* is a very pretty evergreen companion, its lacy, green foliage a nice contrast with the white felty foliage of the *Lychnis coronaria*. The white flowers of the feverfew may echo or contrast with the colorful blooms of the *Lychnis*.

Lychnis coronaria may be used to brighten neglected dry areas of the garden. Since it can survive with no irrigation, rose campion is a good introduced perennial for a native garden. Water it once every 2 weeks for the first summer.

Dwarf barberry *(Berberis)* and *Caryopteris clandonensis* are good companions.

A single specimen is an effective accent. Several plants grouped together are very showy. Use this evergray perennial in a small garden or a large herbaceous border.

PROPAGATION

Lychnis coronaria self-sows so freely that you won't need to think about how to propagate more plants! Young plants may be moved easily to their permanent location in late winter or early spring. Seed should not be covered with compost. If you are spreading a mulch in the fall, allow the seed to fall on top of the mulch. This is a perennial that cannot be divided or propagated vegetatively.

MAINTENANCE

If you have the time to deadhead this freely-blooming perennial, you may be rewarded with more flowers, since the plant will not be putting energy into developing seed. However, the seedpods are attractive with the same gray-white felty appearance, and may be left as part of the textural interest of the branching stalks. Remove faded stalks with winter cleanup.

Lychnis chalcedonica (Maltese cross) has been eaten by the deer in my garden. Other gardeners have reported the same experience.

OENOTHERA

Oenothera tetragona
(sundrops)

Oenothera tetragona

Three of the evening primroses have been tried for deer-resistance in my garden. More commonly referred to as sundrops (which may also be used as a cultivar name), the beautiful herbaceous to semi-evergreen *Oenothera tetragona* has been deer-resistant.

DESCRIPTION

Oenothera tetragona brings three colors into the garden: the beautiful dark-green of its leaves, the red in the stems and fall foliage, and the bright-yellow of its flowers. Crowns establish quickly to an 18-inch width, and the herbaceous plant spreads to a 2-foot height and width. The base of the plant, as it spreads to form new rosettes for next year's stalks, may be evergreen.

Its habit is somewhat sprawling, so give it room unless you plan to provide support.

CULTURAL REQUIREMENTS

Zones 4–10. This lovely plant is a good perennial for even the coldest zones of the western, southwestern, and northwestern United States.

Flowers open only in the brightest light. Full sun, or reflected light from a wall or walk, is the best exposure for sundrops.

Soil should not be rich, but fertility may be increased with the addition of some compost and organic phosphorus. With too much compost, or compost high in nitrogen, growth will be rank and less attractive. A well-composted mulch around the crown is a good cultural practice, and will reduce watering needs.

Oenothera tetragona is fairly drought-tolerant, but will need irrigation every 2 to 3 weeks during the dry summer months in very hot climates.

BLOOM

One of the best of the perennials for bright-yellow flowers, sundrops begins to bloom in early summer, and continues for several weeks. Flowers are slightly cup-shaped, 1½ to 2 inches in diameter (open), and a clear, strong yellow. The contrast with the red stems and dark-green leaves is striking.

As a cut flower, the petals may close when the blossom is brought inside. Place it in the brightest light possible.

SEASONAL INTEREST

Oenothera tetragona is a very attractive plant with a long season of interest because of its colorful red stems, nice foliage and pleasing flowers. Tight basal rosettes of dark-green leaves add winter interest in mild climates.

COMPANION PLANTS AND LANDSCAPE USE

For a striking contrast, the purple flowers of *Verbena venosa* are perfect, and the two plants can sprawl together. Add the Santa Barbara daisy (*Erigeron karvinskianus*), and this will be a focal point in your garden for most of the summer.

Snow-in-summer (*Cerastium tomentosum*), with its gray foliage is a good contrast to the dark-green of the sundrops' leaves. The white flowers are a nice complement to the bright-yellow sundrops.

Lavenders and lavandins are good companions for sundrops, even though they may be watered as often as the sundrops because of their proximity.

PROPAGATION

Propagate *Oenothera tetragona* by taking vegetative cuttings after the first wave of bloom or in very early spring. Divisions may be made in fall from the new rosettes forming near the stalks, or during the dormant season.

MAINTENANCE

EASY! No maintenance is needed until winter. Cut all stalks back to the crown during the dormant season.

Oenothera berlandieri, O. speciosa (Mexican evening primrose) and **Oenothera stricta (O. odorata)** have been eaten by the deer. They love the flowers!

PAEONIA

Paeonia lactiflora
(peony)

The common garden peonies grown in my garden have all been hybrids of the Chinese peony, *Paeonia lactiflora*. While there are other species in this genus, they have not been tested for deer-resistance. One summer out of 27 spent on this garden site, there were six fawns romping around the garden. One peony was sampled repeatedly while their mothers left all the peonies in the garden alone. This is the only time there has been damage to a peony in my garden.

DESCRIPTION

Paeonia is a beautiful herbaceous perennial with large divided leaves varying from mid-green to dark-green. Stems have good color too, some with varying shades of red. Roots are tuberous. An established plant that has not been disturbed will be 3 feet or more in height, and 3 to 4 feet in spread, with a root crown of 18 to 24 inches.

CULTURAL REQUIREMENTS

Zones 2–10. Peonies do much better in cold regions than they do in very warm, mild climates. In the warmer areas of the western United States, peonies may not flower. Knowing your garden's microclimates is important for this perennial. In mild-winter areas, a "cold" spot in your garden in winter, that is in sun by late spring, may work.

Full sun to part shade is the best exposure for *Paeonia* while it is growing. Winter shade may be full shade, since the plant is dormant.

Soil preparation is very important, since this is a long-lived perennial that should not be disturbed. Compost must be well-aged, or low in nitrogen. An active or "hot" compost may damage the roots. Roots are fleshy tubers with fine feeder roots, and "eyes" (somewhat like a potato). Be generous with the addition of an organic phosphorus. Soft rock phosphate is an excellent choice, since it has larger particles which will weather, providing phosphorus for many years.

Prepare planting holes for *Paeonia* 18 inches wide and 18 inches deep for each plant. Place tubers so that the eyes are on top, since this is where growth will originate. It is especially important to cover the eyes with only 1½ inches of compost or soil, including the mulch. Tubers that are planted too deeply may grow beautiful leaves, but seldom flower.

Established peonies are drought-tolerant, but may flower more if irrigated every 2 weeks. A newly-planted peony benefits from being irrigated once every week to 10 days. Avoid overhead irrigation, if possible, when the plant is in bloom.

BLOOM

In late spring, *Paeonia lactiflora* hybrids have strikingly beautiful blossoms in a range of colors from white, through pink and rose, to dark red. Some are one color with markings of a darker color. Most are 4 inches or more in diameter, in forms that vary from single to fully double. Some are fragrant!

All are excellent cut flowers with strong stems. They are also very excellent flowers for floating in water.

Blossoms that collect water may bend with the weight. Irrigate at the base of the plant only, when flowers are opening. In regions where rains are expected, staking systems that will hold the flowers may be necessary.

Each plant opens flowers for about three weeks, depending on the weather. Hot weather in late spring may shorten the bloom.

SEASONAL INTEREST

Paeonia lactiflora has a long season of interest because of its beautiful foliage. With the introduction of different hybrids in your garden, and favorable weather, the bloom period may last for two or more months.

Peony foliage often has good fall color, lasting until winter's chill spells the end of the season.

Paeonia lactiflora

COMPANION PLANTS AND LANDSCAPE USE

Paeonia lactiflora hybrids have several uses in the landscape. Because they do not need irrigation once they are established, they may be used in the dry garden. In drought conditions, the foliage may fade at the end of summer.

Planted in an irrigated herbaceous border, peonies are showy from early spring through fall. The first spring growth is fascinating. Don't miss it! Colorful new shoots emerge early, opening with increasing grace and beauty each day.

Amsonia ciliata and *Ceratostigma willmottianum* are planted near the *Paeonia* in my garden, both for the contrasts in foliage and flower color and form, as well as their beautiful combinations of fall color. And each of these herbaceous perennials has a distinct plant form to add to the border.

Paeonia is a strong structural plant for a large or small garden. A single specimen is striking, a large planting in bloom is breathtaking.

Peonies have many good companions with other sun-loving perennials. Since they may be placed in an irrigated border or in a drier zone, *Paeonia* hybrids are an important perennial in the garden.

Early spring-flowering bulbs may be planted near a peony, but not so close that the peony roots will overtake the bulbs, or be in the way should you want to lift and divide the bulbs. Bulbs should be planted 18 to 24 inches from the center of a peony.

Peonies are beautiful container plants in a large container. Potting soil may need to be renewed after a few years. This should be done during the dormant season. A variety of trailing perennials, such as snow-in-summer *(Cerastium tomentosum)*, or one of the many species and cultivars of creeping thyme *(Thymus)* may be grown at its base, adding winter interest when the peony fades.

PROPAGATION

Peony roots should be left undisturbed. However, if you do want to increase your planting, an established root may be lifted and divided in winter, allowing two to three eyes for each root division. From a division with three eyes, it usually takes one to two years in the ground before the peony will bloom. In five years, the crown will be about 12 inches wide, and you should be rewarded with lots of flowers.

MAINTENANCE

Stake your plants if you are in an area where it rains or snows during the late spring when peonies are in bloom.

Flowering stems may be removed to the crown as soon as the show is over. Cut back faded leaf stalks during winter cleanup.

PAPAVER

Papaver orientale
(oriental poppy)

Papaver orientale

In bloom, oriental poppy is the most exciting perennial in my garden. Visitors exclaim over the huge flowers and vibrant colors. An herbaceous perennial that puts on a show in spring, and then disappears soon after, *Papaver orientale* is worth the fleeting display of grandeur.

DESCRIPTION

A mature oriental poppy has a deep taproot with a crown that is little more than 1 foot wide. The plant may grow to 3 feet in height and width, but the leaves fade soon after bloom. Leaves are large, hairy, and coarse-looking, and form attractive clumps. This is an herbaceous perennial that may die back in the heat of summer in a dry border. Large, spectacular poppies are the pinnacle of its show. *Papaver orientale* is very drought-tolerant.

CULTURAL REQUIREMENTS

Zones 3–9. Success in warmer zones, where oriental poppy may be short-lived, depends on good winter drainage. Plant seedlings or divisions in an area of the garden that will remain in full sun for years, so that plants will not have to be moved. An oriental poppy in less than full sun will have fewer blooms.

Papaver orientale prefers a deeply enriched soil with plenty of compost and organic phosphorus. This poppy will grow in poor soils but does not produce as big a plant or as many flowers as it will in improved soil. Planting holes should be very large, as for peonies.

Oriental poppy is also similar to peonies in its watering requirements, including the need to be watered at the base of the plant when it is in bloom. A deep watering once every two weeks is sufficient, but oriental poppy is known to do well in good soils with less frequent watering. This is a good herbaceous perennial for the dry garden.

Irrigation once a week is tolerated if soil drainage is good.

If old plants have declined, lift the roots when they are dormant, and improve the soil.

BLOOM

Huge poppies to 6 inches or more in diameter are a focal point in the garden in early summer. The colors in my garden include a vibrant red-orange with black markings around the center, a deep peach, also with dark markings, and a white with purple markings. There are many shades of red, orange, and pink, double or single, available in named cultivars.

Blossoms may be used for cut flowers but will need to be heat-treated, with the bottom of the stems quickly seared in a flame or very hot water. Cut flowers do not last long.

Seedpods that follow the faded flowers begin to dry as the foliage fades. These pods are attractive in dried arrangements, with long, very strong stems. If you want seed to mature, do not cut the stems until they are very dry. Seeds are tiny and black, and will shake out of the pods quite easily. One pod supplies more than enough seed for most gardens.

SEASONAL INTEREST

Papaver orientale

Papaver orientale has interesting foliage in spring, with large gray-green leaves that add an unusual texture and strength of form to the border. The leaves appear hairy and bristly.

As the flowering buds begin to emerge, oriental poppy is even more interesting. Watch for the first sign of color as the bud opens, then be sure to check the emerging flower each day, preferably morning and evening! Or better yet, sit by it all day reading a book, and noting the changes from hour to hour!

The season of show is short, with oriental poppy fading very soon after bloom. There will be more flowers next year!

Pods may be left in the border for the interest they add, or cut for winter everlasting bouquets.

COMPANION PLANTS AND LANDSCAPE USE

In many climates, oriental poppy blooms at the same time as peony, and in my garden they are kept separate from one another so that they do not compete.

The strong foliage of the perennial sunflower (*Helianthus maximilianii*) is good contrasting form for the flowers of oriental poppy.

In my garden, black-eyed Susan (*Rudbeckia fulgida* 'Goldsturm') grows very close to *Papaver orientale*. Its dark-green foliage and emerging flower stems divert attention from the fading poppy in midsummer.

Swamp sunflower (*Helianthus angustifolius*) is also an excellent companion since the oriental poppy will tolerate an irrigated border.

In the dry garden, *Iris spuria* and dwarf barberries (*Berberis*) are effective companions.

PROPAGATION

Oriental poppies may be grown from seed, which germinates fairly easily, but it may be 2 to 3 years before the plant will bloom. If you are willing to dig up an established root during the dormant season (late summer or fall), root cuttings will make new plants. This poppy cannot be divided easily.

MAINTENANCE

No maintenance is needed, unless you want to remove the fading foliage and flower stems. In my garden, the leaves simply become part of the summer mulch. All the pods are saved for winter bouquets, but first their seeds are shaken out of the pods and stored in a cool dry place.

PENSTEMON

Penstemon
(penstemon, beard tongue)

Penstemon are among the showiest of wildflowers in North America. Membership in the American Penstemon Society increased my awareness of the hundreds of species from the rocky crevices of the Sierra Nevada and Rocky Mountains to the plains of Nebraska. Most do best right where they are growing, but there are many suitable for the garden. However, not all are deer-resistant. All of these have been good butterfly plants.

Penstemon campanulatus 'Evelyn' and 'Garnet'

DESCRIPTION

Penstemon campanulatus hybrids are bushy evergreen perennials with attractive narrow leaves and very showy flowers. Both are long bloomers for the summer border. 'Evelyn' is the smaller of the two cultivars, with the height and spread of about 2 feet, pink flowers, and light-green leaves. 'Garnet' has a height and spread of 3 or more feet, and wine-red flowers.

CULTURAL REQUIREMENTS

Penstemon campanulatus 'Garnet'

Zones 8–10. Full sun to very light shade is the best exposure. In coastal areas with clouds and fog, place these penstemon in full sun. In the hot inland and foothill regions, some afternoon shade is not necessary, but may extend bloom during the hottest summer months.

As their native habitats would indicate, penstemon grow in a wide variety of soil conditions, and good drainage is more important than soil fertility. Add some well-aged compost to enrich the soil slightly, and be generous with the addition of organic phosphorus (soft rock phosphate). Gravelly soils are appropriate for *Penstemon,* and good winter drainage is essential to ensure their longevity.

Beard tongue thrives in arid climates, but some species get regular rain from thunderstorms during the summer in their native habitat. In my dry-summer climate in the Sierra foothills, summer irrigation every 2 to 3 weeks improves performance.

A mulch will conserve moisture during the dry summer months. Many penstemon grow in regions where summer rain is common.

Penstemon 'Garnet' and 'Evelyn' both will tolerate higher irrigation and wetter clay soils in the winter. Both also do well in an irrigated garden (every 7 to 10 days), or in a dry garden with the irrigation once every 2 to 3 weeks.

BLOOM

Strong stalks hold many tubular flowers, opening from the bottom up. 'Evelyn' is a mid-pink, and 'Garnet' is a rich wine-red. Both will attract hummingbirds and butterflies, though 'Garnet' is the favorite.

Penstemon campanulatus hybrids bloom for several months. Deadhead by removing only the portion of the stalk that has had flowers. It will branch where you have cut it, and more flowering stalks will form through the summer. Additional stalks continue to grow from the crown of the plant, adding to the lengthy show of flowers.

'Evelyn' and 'Garnet' are both excellent cut flowers, and since they will branch where you have cut the stalk, you will have more flowers.

SEASONAL INTEREST

Penstemon campanulatus is an attractive evergreen perennial with a long season of interest. Bloom begins in early summer and extends into fall if plants are deadheaded. This perennial continues to add interest in the border into winter because of its attractive leaves.

COMPANION PLANTS AND LANDSCAPE USE

Penstemon campanulatus 'Garnet'

'Garnet' and 'Evelyn' are good companions for each other, and add a lot of color to the summer border as single specimens in a small garden. Herbaceous borders with several plants are very showy.

Caryopteris clandonensis is a good companion in a garden area watered once every two weeks. While the leaves are similar in form, their gray-green is a nice contrast to the dark green of the penstemon. The blue flowers are effective with both the pink and the wine-red. If you have deadheaded your penstemon, and they are still blooming in late summer, *Caryopteris incana* is an attractive companion.

Coreopsis verticillata 'Moonbeam' or Santa Barbara daisy (*Erigeron karvinskianus*) planted in front of both these penstemons are pleasing companions.

The lacy silver foliage of *Artemisia* 'Powis Castle' is a striking contrast for most of the year.

Penstemon campanulatus 'Garnet' and 'Evelyn' are wonderful container plants when planted in a container that is at least a 3-gallon size.

PROPAGATION

Vegetative cuttings must be taken from terminal buds well before they extend into bloom. While this plant is in bloom with the first flush of color, look for good cutting material in the interior of the plant. There will be even more cutting material once the first blooms have been deadheaded. Cuttings root very quickly, and young plants also grow quickly.

MAINTENANCE

Deadheading will extend bloom, and is worth the time spent. See Bloom.

Penstemon campanulatus 'Garnet' and 'Evelyn' are attractive evergreens, but should be cut back to just a few inches at the end of winter. If they are not cut back, they will sprawl in the coming season, and flowering stalks will not be as strong.

Penstemon eatonii
(firecracker penstemon)

DESCRIPTION

Firecracker penstemon is distinctly different from the two cultivars of *Penstemon campanulatus*. Glossy-green leaves up to 6 inches or more in length are basal. The plant itself is low-growing, under a foot in height and up to 2 feet or more in spread. Very strong, almost leafless, flower stalks 2 to 3 feet in height hold tubular mid-scarlet flowers.

CULTURAL REQUIREMENTS

Zones 2–9. This beautiful evergreen penstemon will grow in the coldest regions of the western, southwestern, and northwestern United States as long as it has good winter drainage in heavy soils.

Full hot sun is the best exposure. Reflected heat from rocks or a building will provide the extra heat that this beard tongue requires if it's grown in one of the climates with cooler summers. Even where summers are hot, Penstemon eatonii thrives in the hottest exposure.

Soil does not need to be rich, but may be aerated with the addition of very aged compost. A generous supply of organic phosphorus with the soil preparation will ensure a good root system and an abundance of flowers.

Firecracker penstemon is drought-tolerant, and will survive with irrigation once every 2 to 3 weeks once it is established. Natural rainfall is sufficient in many garden microclimates.

BLOOM

Very attractive scarlet flowers about 1 to 1½ inches in length open along strong, glossy-green stalks. The hummingbirds visit these tubular flowers frequently. The bloom period lasts for a few weeks in midsummer.

Hummingbirds even come into the nursery to sample these blossoms. Firecracker penstemon is an excellent cut flower.

SEASONAL INTEREST

Penstemon eatonii is an outstanding perennial in bloom. The plant is also very attractive, but because it is so low growing, it should be used toward the front of a border. Do not allow neighboring plants to overshadow it.

COMPANION PLANTS AND LANDSCAPE USE

Caryopteris clandonensis is a good companion. Plant the firecracker penstemon near the base of the *Caryopteris*, about 3 feet between crown centers. Depending on your microclimates, the two perennials may be in bloom at the same time. And even if they are not, the strongly vertical stalks and scarlet flowers of the firecracker penstemon are attractive with the gray-green leaves of the *Caryopteris.*

Firecracker penstemon is also very attractive growing near *Artemisia* 'Powis Castle' and feverfew *(Tanacetum parthenium).*

In a small garden, a single specimen is a focal point in bloom, and an attractive smaller evergreen. A drift of firecracker penstemon in a larger garden seems to glow with color.

Penstemon eatonii may be grown in a container.

PROPAGATION

Vegetative cuttings may be taken from terminal buds in early spring, or in late summer after the wave of bloom has passed.

MAINTENANCE

Deadhead flowering stalks by removing the entire stalk to the crown of the plant once the flowers fade. This will encourage a mature plant to produce more flowers. Later stalks may be shorter.

This beautiful evergreen needs no maintenance, other than to remove the occasional spent leaf. Very EASY!

Penstemon hirsutus
(hairy penstemon)

DESCRIPTION

Penstemon hirsutus is a low-growing evergreen, forming an attractive mound up to 18 inches in width, and under a foot in height. The hairy leaves are dark green with a purple cast, up to 5 inches in length, and basal. Multiple flower stalks up to 8 inches in height hold masses of tubular flowers with interesting markings.

CULTURAL REQUIREMENTS

Zones 4–9. *Penstemon hirsutus* will do well in the cold regions of the western, southwestern, and northwestern United States.

Exposure, soil requirements, and irrigation are the same as for *Penstemon companulatus.*

BLOOM

Penstemon hirsutus 'Pygmaeus' has pastel purple flowers on purple stems to 8 inches in height. The white *Penstemon hirsutus* in my garden has green stems. There is also a variation with pink flowers. These 1-inch tubular flowers add a soft effect to the border.

The flowers have a slight nodding habit, and the stalks are strong but not rigid, resulting in movement with the slightest breeze.

Penstemon hirsutus is an early summer bloomer, with most of the flowers opening for several weeks. If it is deadheaded, it will continue to bloom into midsummer, but more sparsely.

SEASONAL INTEREST

While *Penstemon hirsutus* is not as strong an evergreen as *Penstemon eatonii,* its mix of purple and green foliage is attractive year-round. Some leaves may be damaged by winter snows, but they can easily be removed.

The early-summer bloom period is very strong and will continue for a month or more.

COMPANION PLANTS AND LANDSCAPE USE

The low, compact growth habit of hairy penstemon makes it a beautiful plant for the front of the border, or as an accent in the rock garden. The soft pastel shades of the flowers allow it to be used with any other color (even orange!).

A single specimen is a focal point in the small garden, and a mass of several plants as a border edging is quite beautiful.

Planted under the arching leaves of angel's fishing pole (*Dierama pulcherrimum*), the colors and nodding habit of the flowers are echoed by the *Penstemon hirsutus.* The leaves and the two plants' growth habit are distinctly different, which makes the subtle similarities of their flowers even more enchanting.

Use *Penstemon hirsutus* in a container. It's a beauty!

PROPAGATION

Penstemon hirsutus self-sows easily, and in my garden where the white and purple are growing in close proximity, there has been no crossing of colors. Seed-save to increase your plantings, sowing the seed on the soil surface in early spring. Seed will be mature when pods are dry, and you do not need more than a few pods for a plentiful supply of seed.

MAINTENANCE

Removing faded flower stalks by cutting them back to the crown will extend the bloom season. If the evergreen leaves begin to look spent, remove them at the base. This perennial is very EASY!

Penstemon pinifolius

In my nursery and garden, this evergreen perennial has been considered an excellent choice for the rock garden. But several years ago, during the Perennial Plant Association symposium in Denver, in one of the gardens visited, a very large planting of the scarlet *Penstemon pinifolius* caught my attention, and convinced me that this perennial is not only for the rock garden.

DESCRIPTION

Penstemon pinifolius is a very small subshrub, sometimes called a shrublet. Very delicate, tiny mid-green leaves cover the soft stems which grow from a woody base. Grown in a dry rock garden, the plant is usually under a foot tall and wide. With irrigation and in very fertile soil, *Penstemon pinifolius* may grow to 18 inches or more.

CULTURAL REQUIREMENTS

Zones 2–9. This fine perennial will grow in the coldest and the most mild regions of the western, southwestern, and northwestern United States. As long as it has good winter drainage, it will be a long-lasting perennial.

Full sun to part shade is the best exposure. Because this plant is evergreen, it should not be in winter shade where the soil is more likely to remain wet.

As noted, a more fertile soil will result in a larger plant. The addition of organic compost and phosphorus is a good idea, but think about how big you want the plant to grow.

Penstemon pinifolius is drought-tolerant. Irrigation may be once every 2 to 3 weeks, or more often.

BLOOM

Small, tubular scarlet flowers under 1 inch in length, are exquisite with the fine foliage. 'Mersea Yellow' has yellow flowers, an unusual color in the *Penstemon* genus.

Deadhead faded flowers by cutting back the portion that has bloomed, leaving the leafy stalk below. The stems will continue to branch, and more flowers will form. Bloom begins in midsummer and may continue until the end of summer.

SEASONAL INTEREST

The delicate appearance of this perennial is attractive year-round. While the flowers are an obvious asset in the garden, the worth of this plant is also its unusual foliage. So many stems are formed that *Penstemon pinifolius* does look like a miniature evergreen shrub.

For several weeks, strong color, either scarlet or bright yellow, adds to the garden.

COMPANION PLANTS AND LANDSCAPE USE

In a rock garden, *Penstemon pinifolius* is a focal point wherever it is planted. In a larger herbaceous border, it is still a standout in bloom, but its smaller size makes it a good edging plant.

Use scarlet *Penstemon pinifolius* against the silver foliage of *Artemisia* 'Powis Castle' or snow-in-summer (*Cerastium tomentosum*) nearby.

Caryopteris clandonensis is a good companion for either the scarlet or the yellow, with the *Penstemon pinifolius* growing at its base. Add mountain bluet (*Centaurea montana*) next to the *Caryopteris* and behind the *Penstemon pinifolius*.

This delicate beard tongue is also an excellent container plant or an accent in a small garden.

PROPAGATION

Each plant provides an ample supply of terminal buds for vegetative cuttings, even when it is in bloom. Focus on the growth in the center of the plant since it is less likely to develop flowers.

MAINTENANCE

Remove faded flowers from *Penstemon pinifolius* by cutting back only the portion of the stalk that has bloomed.

Before new growth starts in the spring, cut back all of last season's growth to a small woody structure under 4 inches in height.

Penstemon strictus
(Rocky Mountain penstemon)

DESCRIPTION

The plant of *Penstemon strictus* is very similar to *Penstemon eatonii*, with green glaucous foliage, an attractive evergreen for the garden border. Dark-green leaves up to 6 inches in length form rosettes. Plants are about 18 inches in width, and under a foot in height. Flower stalks rise up to 2 to 3 feet, with beautiful blue flowers.

CULTURAL REQUIREMENTS

Same as for *Penstemon eatonii*.

BLOOM

Very strong stalks hold tubular flowers up to 1½ inches in length, a combination of dark to a very bright blue-purple. This is a very beautiful perennial in bloom, but sadly, the length of bloom is altogether too short. In my hot climate, *Penstemon strictus* rarely blooms for more than three weeks.

SEASONAL INTEREST

Same as for *Penstemon eatonii*.

COMPANION PLANTS AND LANDSCAPE USE

Same as for *Penstemon eatonii*.

PROPAGATION

Same as for *Penstemon eatonii*.

MAINTENANCE

Same as for *Penstemon eatonii*.

Penstemon gloxinoides (garden penstemon hybrids): 'Big Red', 'Huntington Pink', 'Holly's White', 'Sour Grapes', 'Midnight', and 'Lady Hindley' have all been eaten by the deer.

PEROVSKIA

Perovskia atriplicifolia
(Russian sage)

Native from Afghanistan to Tibet, *Perovskia* is one of the best of the mid and late-summer perennials. While it is semi-evergreen (evergray) in some climates, each year the show of foliage, graceful stems and glowing blue-violet flowers is on the new growth.

DESCRIPTION

Graceful stems, 3 to 4 feet in height, with small gray leaves, lean outwardly and arch inwardly. Given the space it requires, the branching stems of *Perovskia atriplicifolia* spread to 4 feet or more. Small, blue-violet flowers open along gray stems, a lovely contrast. The crown of a mature Russian sage is under 2 feet in width.

CULTURAL REQUIREMENTS

Zones 2–10. Russian sage will grow in the coldest regions of the western, southwestern, and northwestern United States.

Its requirements are simple: full hot sun, low irrigation, and soil that is not too fertile. If these requirements are met, *Perovskia atriplicifolia* will be a beautiful plant in the dry border.

Crowded by other plants, Russian sage will not develop to its full potential. If it is overwatered, leaves will yellow. And if soil is too fertile, flowering stems will not be as strong. Organic mulch or gravel mulch may be used to conserve moisture in the soil. Reflected heat from a wall or walkway is beneficial.

If soil has good drainage, this tough perennial may be watered once every two to three weeks.

BLOOM

Perovskia atriplicifolia

Numerous small blue-violet flowers open along the slender silvery-gray stems. As flowers mature, they look puffy, and continue to hold color even as they fade. The spires have a delicate appearance.

Flowering begins in midsummer and continues through fall if plants are deadheaded. Remove only the portion that has bloomed so that the *Perovskia* will continue to branch and form more flowers.

Russian sage is an excellent cut flower, and the flowering sprays may also be dried for winter bouquets by cutting them when the flowers are first opening, and color is strongest.

SEASONAL INTEREST

Perovskia atriplicifolia has a very long season of interest, because the delicate branches look good in the winter landscape, long after the summer and fall flowers have faded. In some climates, the leaves are evergray.

Russian sage blooms for several weeks if it is deadheaded. A few sprays dried for everlastings add another season of interest.

COMPANION PLANTS AND LANDSCAPE USE

Perovskia should never be planted where it is crowded by other plants. Lower perennials grown near the base are good companions if they are not too close (keep a respectful 3 to 4-foot separation). Taller perennials too close to the Russian sage will alter its appearance.

Near the base, Santa Barbara daisy *(Erigeron karvinskianus)*, the low threadleaf coreopsis *(Coreopsis verticillata* 'Moonbeam', or creeping germander *(Teucrium cossonii majoricum)* are all good choices for companions. Even the more aggressively spreading *Verbena venosa* is a good low companion. Low companions may sprawl into the base of the *Perovskia*.

Attentive to the spread of each perennial, *Penstemon* 'Garnet' is a wonderful companion. The center of the *Perovskia* should be placed 3 to 4 feet from the center of the penstemon. In this vast region between the two plants when they are young, scatter a few larkspur *(Consolida ambigua)* seeds for a filler that will not overshadow either perennial.

The dark-blue of *Caryopteris incana*, planted with the penstemon and *Perovskia* combination at a safe distance, is a good addition. Low-irrigation ornamental grasses such as feather grass *(Stipa tenuissima)* or blue gamma grass *(Bouteloua gracilis)* are also perfect companions.

PROPAGATION

Do not attempt to divide the crown of *Perovskia*. Take vegetative cuttings early in the spring, or during the summer from side shoots, well before they extend into bloom. Cuttings root very quickly.

MAINTENANCE

Deadhead during the summer bloom when color has passed by removing only the portion of the stem that has bloomed.

Russian sage does not need to be staked when it is given plentiful sun and enough space to grow naturally. Part of the beauty of this perennial is its form, which is lost when stakes are used to hold the plant rigidly upright.

In some climates, *Perovskia atriplicifolia* is evergray, with a woody structure. At the end of winter, cut last year's branches to buds that are about 4 to 6 inches from the crown.

PHLOMIS

Phlomis russeliana
(Jerusalem sage)

The deer pass by this robust evergreen perennial, though the rough, hairy leaves of *Phlomis* resemble those of comfrey, which they always eat. This is fortunate, since *Phlomis russeliana* is an unusual structural plant in my garden.

DESCRIPTION

Large dark-green leaves, to 8 inches in length are heart-shaped and basal in growth habit, forming rosettes that spread by runners to establish large clumps 3 to 4 feet in width, and 1 foot to 18 inches in height. Very stiff and erect 3-foot stems hold ball-shaped whorls of yellow flowers.

CULTURAL REQUIREMENTS

Zones 4–10. Jerusalem sage will not grow in the coldest regions, though it will tolerate winter temperatures to 10°F. In my garden, winter cold and snows have done no damage.

Full sun to part shade are good exposures in coastal climates. In the hot foothills and valleys, some afternoon shade is preferred.

Soil preparation is important, and the addition of an organic compost and phosphorus will ensure a healthy, attractive plant. Mulch with more compost each year. In less fertile soils, *Phlomis russeliana* will be smaller, with weaker stalks.

Jerusalem sage does well in the dry shade garden as long as the soil is fertile. In areas with no summer rains, in midsummer heat, irrigation every two weeks is sufficient.

BLOOM

The individual flowers are tubular and yellow. Many of them are bunched tightly together, forming a ball. Each flowering stalk supports three to four of these clusters, surrounding the stem. The effect is quite striking. This is a good cut flower.

Do not deadhead. The form is still interesting as flowers fade.

SEASONAL INTEREST

Because it is evergreen, *Phlomis* is an attractive addition to the border throughout the year. With large leaves, the effect in the winter border is strong.

Phlomis also adds strong vertical interest with its stalks, and the flowers are intriguing. The combination of leaves, plant form, stalk, and flower clusters is unusual, and worthy of a place in any garden.

COMPANION PLANTS AND LANDSCAPE USE

Since we cannot enjoy *Hosta* in deer country, *Phlomis russeliana* supplies an evergreen with bold leaves for the shade garden. It is more drought-tolerant in shade than *Hosta,* and more adaptable to an arid climate such as mine!

Combine Jerusalem sage with maiden grass (*Miscanthus sinensis* 'Morning Light' or 'Adagio'). The contrasts of these two perennials include leaf form and color, plant form, and flower form and color.

The leaves of lady's mantle (*Alchemilla mollis*) are a pleasing contrast, and the flowers a color echo. Refer to *Alchemilla mollis* for more pleasing companions.

Ladybells (*Adenophora confusa*) has blue flowers that are a pleasing contrast with the yellow Jerusalem sage.

Phlomis russeliana is effective in a small garden as an accent, in a larger border as a single specimen, and in plantings where several plants make an even bolder statement.

PROPAGATION

In winter, established clumps may be divided by lifting the entire plant, or by digging into the crown to remove sections that have formed from runners.

MAINTENANCE

EASY! Remove leaves that are unattractive at any time, cutting them back to the crown. Remove stalks when you don't like how they look! Cut them back to the crown.

Romneya coulteri

ROMNEYA

Romneya coulteri
(Matilija poppy, fried-egg plant)

One of the most beautiful perennials in my garden, *Romneya coulteri* is a native of Southern California, but grows in the coldest regions of the western United States. These evergreens spread to establish large stands of spectacular white poppies.

DESCRIPTION

Matilija poppy has bluish gray-green foliage along the stalks, with showy white poppies forming at the top. In my garden plants are 4 to 5 tall, but they may reach as tall as 7 feet. Spread is aggressive with underground rhizomes, and new plants may emerge a few feet away from the parent plant.

CULTURAL REQUIREMENTS

Zones, 7–10. *Romneya coulteri* will grow in the coldest regions of the western, southwestern, and northwestern United States. If your region has very cold winters, try growing this perennial near a south-facing wall.

Full sun is the best exposure, but there are wild stands in the Sierra Nevada foothills with only a western exposure to sun. Planted in an eastern exposure (shade after 3 p.m.) on my property, Matilija poppy has grown very well but does not seem to have as many flowers as those grown in full sun.

Soil should not be rich. *Romneya* grows well in either sandy or clay soils. The addition of a small amount of compost and organic phosphorus is appropriate to get this plant established. Once it begins growth, the roots will reach into adjacent soil areas where there has been no soil improvement. Even rocks do not stop the growth of this plant.

Romneya needs no irrigation once it has established, but it will tolerate occasional (every 3 to 4 weeks) irrigation or summer rainfall. When plants are young, water occasionally when leaves droop (learn this by feeling a hydrated leaf: it will be firmer), but not as often as you would irrigate most young perennials.

Watering mature plants once a month will not damage this drought-tolerant perennial, but may encourage it to spread even more! Overwatering may kill *Romneya coulteri*.

BLOOM

The flowers are spectacular. Fried-egg plant is an appropriate description. The center is golden, about 2 inches across, a mass of stamens loaded with pollen. The huge white petals are like crepe paper. Flowers may be as large as 9 inches in diameter. Bees love this flower.

Flowering begins in early summer. The first wave of bloom is the most spectacular and lasts for several weeks. The showy blooms continue to open into late summer, though flowers are fewer by midsummer.

Removing faded flowers may extend and increase the later bloom. The plant will not be putting its energy into forming seed.

Flowers are excellent cut with long stems, or with a short stem, floating the blossom in water.

SEASONAL INTEREST

These evergreen plants are very attractive even when they are not in bloom. A single flower is breathtaking, so the summer interest of this outstanding perennial is strong.

The gray-green foliage adds interest to the winter garden.

COMPANION PLANTS AND LANDSCAPE USE

In the wild garden, stands of Matilija poppy leave room for little else to grow. However, in the garden setting, unwanted plants may be removed if they begin to crowd companions.

Achillea filipendulina is a perfect companion, its golden blossoms an echo of the center of the poppy. Taller *Artemisia* are also good companions, their silvery foliage in contrast to the bluish gray-green of the Matilija poppy.

Iris spuria is an excellent companion plant, contrasting in foliage form and color, and the flowers an echo of the *Romneya's* white.

Russian sage (*Perovskia atriplicifolia*) is another low-irrigation perennial that is a good companion plant for *Romneya*. Its delicate flower spires are definitely a contrast to the showy poppies, and the blue-violet is pleasing with the white. *Perovskia* will do most of its blooming while the *Romneya* has only a few flowers.

Barberries (*Berberis thunbergii*), with their dark-red foliage and rounded form, are a good contrasting shrub. Upright rosemary (*Rosmarinus officinalis*), with its rich, dark-green foliage, is an excellent evergreen companion.

Large drifts of daffodils (*Narcissus* species) are good companions.

PROPAGATION

Romneya coulteri is best propagated by lifting new plants as they form from the underground rhizomes. Take them up as soon as new shoots emerge from the ground in spring. Include a good length of the fleshy root that connects the shoot to the parent plant. It is very difficult to transplant this perennial, and also difficult to grow it in containers. Plants should always be placed in the garden in their permanent location, and left undisturbed if possible.

Seed germination is even more difficult. Burn pine needles on top of the seed bed. After this heat treatment, and a cold period in winter, a few seeds may germinate in spring.

MAINTENANCE

EASY! Remove the faded flowers by cutting back just the portion that has bloomed, or wait for winter cleanup.

At the end of winter, cut the woody stalks back to the ground. This will make a tidier plant for the new season.

On steep banks, plants may be left alone. New growth will cover the old stalks. In areas of mild winters, *Romneya* may be evergray.

ROSMARINUS

Rosmarinus officinalis
(rosemary)

Upright rosemary is a very attractive evergreen subshrub, a Mediterranean plant that thrives in hot, dry locations where winter temperatures are above 10° F. Both the upright and the trailing cultivars include some that are not hardy in colder temperatures. Listed in this section are those cultivars which have done well with winter temperatures to 6°F.

DESCRIPTION

Rosmarinus officinalis 'Beneden Blue' and 'Arp' are upright cultivars 3 to 4 feet in height and spread. 'Arp' has finer leaves, giving it a more delicate appearance than 'Beneden Blue'. Narrow leaves are rich, dark-green and thickly borne on upright branching stalks. Blue flowers begin opening in midwinter. The trailing forms of rosemary are about 18 inches in height, and may spread as much as 6 to 8 feet. 'Lockewood de Forest' is the best cultivar of trailing rosemary for very cold regions.

CULTURAL REQUIREMENTS

Zones 8–10. If you are gardening in regions or microclimates where winter temperatures may be expected to fall to 10°F or below freezing, plant the cultivars suggested, since they have been proven to be hardy to 6° F. Other cultivars are certainly worth trying, but may be damaged or killed by winter temperatures below 15°F.

Full sun is the best exposure for rosemary, and it will thrive in a western exposure with morning shade and afternoon sun, even in the Sierra foothills where summer temperatures may stay above 100°F for several days. *Rosmarinus officinalis* also does quite well in morning sun and afternoon shade.

Rosemary does not need rich soil, but the addition of organic phosphorus and compost is still important, in sandy or clay soils.

No irrigation is needed once rosemary is established, but it will tolerate irrigation once every 1 to 2 weeks, depending on your soil. In heavy clays, which hold moisture longer, rosemary must have good drainage to survive. If you are including it in a planting with more frequent irrigation, allow for good drainage both in summer and in winter. Rosemary is a good plant for rocky or gravelly soils.

BLOOM

Rosmarinus officinalis

Small blue flowers vary in color from dark-blue to light lilac-blue. They open within the foliage on the stalks. In some areas, where winters are mild, *Rosmarinus officinalis* may begin bloom in December, and continue bloom into late spring.

Flowers attract bees, butterflies, and the occasional hummingbird.

Cut sprays are excellent in floral arrangements. Flowers will not hold up if rosemary is cut and dried, but cut the foliage for baths and cooking.

SEASONAL INTEREST

Rosmarinus officinalis is a plant of year-round beauty and interest. It is also edible. Chefs have their favorite cultivars. Mine is 'Beneden Blue' because the stalks are so thick with leaves. Only a few inches are removed from the plant to have an ample supply for cooking.

A handsome plant in the winter garden, rosemary is one of those plants that may not be noticed much during the spring and summer display of perennials. When the rich green stalks are showing above 2 feet of snow, it is suddenly the focal point of the garden.

COMPANION PLANTS AND LANDSCAPE USE

Common sage (*Salvia officinalis*) has several forms, all of which are excellent companions. Nice contrasts of foliage and form. One of the many species and cultivars of thyme (*Thymus*) completes the picture.

Upright rosemary is compatible with other drought-resistant plants, such as Matilija poppy (*Romneya coulteri*), *Achillea filipendulina* 'Coronation Gold', and all of the *Santolina* species.

Rosmarinus officinalis may also be used in a higher irrigation border as long as the drainage is good, especially in winter. Black-eyed Susan (*Rudbeckia fulgida* 'Goldsturm') is a striking companion. *Caryopteris clandonensis* adds a bit of gray to this combination with its gray-green leaves.

There are several ornamental grasses which are very effective with upright rosemary. My favorites include blue gamma grass (*Bouteloua gracilis*), feather grass (*Stipa tenuissima*), and dwarf maiden grass (*Miscanthus sinensis* 'Adagio').

Rosemary is a good container plant in a large container that is at least 5 gallons.

PROPAGATION

Vegetative cuttings are easily taken from rosemary because of its branching habit. Cuttings may be taken from early spring into fall and will root quickly. This is true of both the upright and the prostrate cultivars.

Older plants may also be layered. With a rock or a groundcloth staple, anchor a branch to the ground where it bends close, then cover the union of stem and ground with compost. Once this section has formed roots, it may be cut from the parent plant, cut back to a few inches height, and planted out into the garden.

MAINTENANCE

Very EASY! Prune rosemary as needed to shape the plant and encourage it to branch. If any branches are affected by winter cold, just remove them back to healthy wood.

RUDBECKIA

Rudbeckia fulgida 'Goldsturm'
(black-eyed Susan)

Rudbeckia fulgida 'Goldsturm'

Rudbeckia adds gold and yellow to the summer border with large daisies of striking beauty. The deer will eat *Rudbeckia nitida* and *Rudbeckia triloba*, but they never touch *Rudbeckia fulgida* 'Goldsturm' in my garden.

DESCRIPTION

This herbaceous perennial spreads by stolons to form thick mats of dark-green leaves up to 8 inches in length. Size of the leaves will depend on the soil fertility. Out of bloom this perennial is about 1 foot in height. Branching stalks support multiple golden daisies in summer.

CULTURAL REQUIREMENTS

Zones 2–10. Black-eyed Susan does well in the coldest regions of the western, southwestern, and northwestern United States.

Rudbeckia grows in full sun to partial shade. In hot climates, a little shade may make the individual flowers last longer. Reflected heat from a building or walkway may shorten the bloom.

Enrich soil with an ample supply of organic compost and phosphorus. This perennial will not perform in poor soils. Mulch thickly (2 to 3 inches deep) with organic materials such as decomposed straw mixed with compost.

Regular irrigation once a week is best, but a mature *Rudbeckia fulgida* with a good mulch may survive with the irrigation only once every 2 weeks, if it gets a little afternoon shade.

BLOOMS

Golden daisies 3 to 4 inches in diameter open on branching stalks for several weeks. Microclimates will determine when bloom starts. A warm microclimate will stimulate black-eyed Susan to open in early summer. *Rudbeckia fulgida* 'Goldsturm' usually begins bloom in midsummer, and continues for two months. At the peak of bloom, a wave of gold almost blankets the view of the dark green foliage.

Do not rush to deadhead. The seedheads that follow the fading blooms are very beautiful for months.

Black-eyed Susan is an excellent cut flower. Also cut a few sprays with seedheads for winter everlastings.

SEASONAL INTEREST

In early spring, the handsome dark-green leaves are a welcome strength in a herbaceous border. As they grow larger, their beauty adds to the garden long before stalks form for bloom.

By late spring and early summer, branching stalks add a texture and the promise of color.

Flowers open for several weeks in summer. Seedheads that follow continue the seasonal interest through fall.

Rudbeckia fulgida 'Goldsturm' is dormant in winter.

COMPANION PLANTS AND LANDSCAPE USE

With attention to its requirements for regular irrigation, black-eyed Susan combines beautifully with many other perennials. In bloom at the same time as Shasta daisies, it is about the same height as the cultivar 'Silver Princess'. The dwarf cultivars of Shasta daisy, 'Little Miss Muffet' or 'Snow Lady' may be used in front of the black-eyed Susan. Swamp sunflower *(Helianthus angustifolius)* is a good companion. The leaves are the same rich dark-green, but they differ in shape, and the form of the two plants is distinctly different. The *Helianthus* will flower after the black-eyed Susan.

Santa Barbara daisy *(Erigeron karvinskianus)* is an excellent companion, its delicate foliage and flowers a sweet contrast to the strong foliage and flowers of the black-eyed Susan. Remembering that *Rudbeckia fulgida* 'Goldsturm' is an enthusiastic spreader, plant the Santa Barbara daisy at least 3 to 4 feet distant from the crown center of 'Goldsturm'.

Black-eyed Susan is a very attractive container plant for medium (2-gallon) to large (5-gallon or more) containers. The larger the container, the more years the perennial may be left undisturbed.

PROPAGATION

Rudbeckia fulgida 'Goldsturm' is easiest to divide in the fall when young plants with roots have formed at the end of the stolons. At this stage, very little of the crown will need to be disturbed. It is much more difficult to divide in the spring without digging into the crown of the plant. Sections of the crown may also be lifted carefully with a good garden fork, and pulled apart. Always include some roots. Young plants should be attached to a rooted section.

MAINTENANCE

Very EASY! With winter cleanup, remove faded stalks and leaves to the crown. If you procrastinate in doing this job, you may need to remove only stalks, as the leaves have become part of the mulch.

Rudbeckia nitida (golden glow) flowers are favored by the deer, and they will also browse on its foliage. Grown surrounded by other perennials or by ornamental grasses, this Rudbeckia may be left alone. The deer like the flowers, so keep them out of reach!

Rudbeckia triloba (wild black-eyed Susan) reaches 3 feet in height in my garden, and then is trimmed back by the deer to about 2 feet. It usually grows again to 3 feet (untouched, to 4 feet) and blooms with multiple small black-eyed Susans. The deer seem to prefer the young foliage to the flowers.

Ruta graveolens

Ruta graveolens
(rue)

The blue-green foliage of *Ruta graveolens* glows in the winter landscape. One of the most attractive of evergreen subshrubs, it is seldom seen in gardens. This wonderful perennial should be one of the most important plants in deer country.

DESCRIPTION

Rue is an evergreen that includes several cultivars, all with similar blue-green leaves, but varying height and spread. The leaflets are small, their arrangement fernlike. They are very aromatic when brushed. One of the larger rues, the cultivar 'Jackman's Blue' is 3 to 4 feet in height and spread. 'Blue Mound' is smaller, with an 18-inch height and spread. The flowers are yellow, opening in early summer.

CULTURAL REQUIREMENTS

Zones 4–10. *Ruta graveolens* will grow in the coldest regions of the western, southwestern, and northwestern United States.

Sun to partial shade is the best exposure for rue. In partial shade, rue is more drought-tolerant.

Improve the soil slightly with the addition of compost and phosphorus, but do not create a rich soil for this tough herb.

While *Ruta graveolens* is drought-tolerant, its appearance is more attractive when it is irrigated at least once a month. Because it needs very little water in shade, this is a good evergreen perennial for the dry shade garden. Rue will tolerate higher irrigation, especially in a sunny location, but do not overwater. If the soil drainage is good, rue may be watered every two weeks. Foliage will begin to turn yellow, especially the lower leaves, if it is getting too much water.

In very cold cimates, mulch with straw in winter.

BLOOM

Yellow flowers are single, in clusters on branching stalks. They are not showy, but are attractive with the blue-green foliage.

Sprays may be used for cut flowers, but the odor will be intense for the first day or two. The same is true of the foliage, which is beautiful in winter bouquets. But don't bring it inside until the strength of the odor lessens a couple of days after cutting.

Bloom lasts for a few weeks from early to midsummer. Deadhead the entire stalk when bloom has faded.

SEASONAL INTEREST

Ruta graveolens is a beautiful evergreen for year-round interest in any garden. Its lacy foliage and slight movement with a breeze add a soft effect.

The color of the foliage is unusual in winter, and seems to glow. Often unnoticed during the glory of spring and summer-blooming perennials, *Ruta graveolens* becomes a focal point in the winter landscape.

COMPANION PLANTS AND LANDSCAPE USE

Rue is very beautiful with rosemary, or any other perennial with dark-green foliage. Black-eyed Susan (*Rudbeckia fulgida* 'Goldsturm') is a good companion in light shade, with the irrigation once every two weeks.

Feverfew (*Tanacetum parthenium*) is effective with rue. Though both have similar lacy foliage, the rue is blue-green and the feverfew bright to dark-green. Both are evergreen.

Use *Ruta graveolens* as an evergreen near ornamental grasses such as *Miscanthus sinensis* 'Morning Light' or 'Adagio'. As the grass foliage turns golden, the blue-green rue foliage is a dynamic contrast. These companions take the fall interest right into winter.

All of the *Santolina* species and cultivars are good companion plants.

Rue is a good container plant, but because its root system is large, the container must be at least 5 gallons for a mature plant.

PROPAGATION

Take vegetative cuttings from terminal buds beginning in spring. Because these cuttings are slow to root, take vegetative cuttings through the summer months, but not in fall. It is difficult for unrooted cuttings to winter-over even in a protected location such as a cold frame.

MAINTENANCE

Very EASY! *Ruta graveolens* needs little maintenance. A light shearing at the end of winter will stimulate new growth and define the shape of this subshrub. Deadheading consists of removing a few stalks with fading flower sprays.

Salvia officinalis

Salvia
(sage)

There are many *Salvia*, but not all are hardy, or deer-resistant. A gardener just down the hill from me has been able to grow *Salvia greggii*, while my garden site is too cold in winter. In my garden, *Salvia chamaedryoides* and *Salvia officinalis* (sage) have been the best evergreen (evergray) subshrubs in this genus, and the deer will not eat either species. *Salvia officinalis* and its cultivars are excellent herbs for cooking.

DESCRIPTION

Salvia chamaedryoides is an evergray subshrub with small silvery leaves on silvery stems, and brilliant blue flowers. It grows to 2 feet in height and 3 feet in spread.

Salvia officinalis is the common evergray sage, 2 to 3 feet (in bloom) in height, and 3 to 4 feet in spread. Flowers are blue-violet.

Salvia officinalis 'Nana' is a dwarf evergray cultivar, 18 inches to 2 feet in height and 2 to 3 feet in spread. Flower stalks and flowers are smaller than the species, the same shade of blue.

Salvia officinalis 'Berggarten' is a non-blooming evergray cultivar with rounded leaves, the same size as *Salvia officinalis*.

Salvia officinalis 'Purpurascens' has purplish tints to the evergray foliage and is the same size as *Salvia officinalis*. It is not as hardy as the other cultivars. *Salvia* 'Tricolor' has gray and purplish-pink evergray foliage with a little white, and is even more tender in cold winters. Temperatures below 25°F will affect these two cultivars.

CULTURAL REQUIREMENTS

Salvia officinalis 'Purpurascens'

Salvia chamaedryoides is a good subshrub in my zone 8a in the Sierra Nevada foothills. However, in this region, it may not survive in very cold microclimates in a cold winter, below 20°F.

Salvia officinalis, with the exception of the two cultivars 'Purpurescens' and 'Tricolor', will grow in the coldest regions of the western, southwestern, and northwestern United States.

The best exposure is full sun to very light shade for *Salvia officinalis* and its cultivars. *Salvia chamaedryoides* does best in full, hot sun and even reflected heat from rocks or a building.

Soil should not be rich, but the addition of compost will improve its tilth, and ensure good drainage. Also, the addition of organic phosphorus is always important for good root development and bloom.

All of these *Salvia* are drought-tolerant and may be used in the dry garden. They also tolerate irrigation once every three to four weeks.

BLOOM

Blue-violet flowers are two-lipped, clustered around the stalk of *Salvia officinalis* in whorls. It flowers heavily in early summer, and if deadheaded, will continue to produce a few flowering stalks into fall. The fading flower stalks are interesting and do not need to be removed if you would prefer to have this texture in the late summer and fall garden.

Salvia chamaedryoides flowers are similar in form, but spaced separately along the stalk. The small flowers are very brilliant blue, and in contrast to the almost silver-white of the foliage, are quite striking. Bloom begins in midsummer and continues until hard frost. Deadhead the portion that has bloomed to encourage branching, and more flowering.

SEASONAL INTEREST

Since all the sages mentioned here are evergreen (or evergray), their season of interest is year-round. *Salvia officinalis* and its cultivars have a well-defined form, which is more noticeable in the winter landscape than the open branching habit of *Salvia chamaedryoides*.

COMPANION PLANTS AND LANDSCAPE USE

All of these sages are strong plants in the rock garden. As evergreens, they have considerable value for any garden.

Upright rosemary (*Rosmarinus officinalis*) is a striking companion year-round.

Verbena venosa, with its dark-green foliage and purple flowers, is an attractive and equally tough companion. In my garden, the *Verbena* grows into the sage, a happy pair. Combine this verbena with *Salvia officinalis* 'Purpurascens' for a great color echo.

Low-irrigation ornamental grasses such as fescues (*Festuca*), blue gamma grass (*Bouteloua gracilis*), and feather grass (*Stipa tenuissima*) play a nice light texture against the foliage of *Salvia officinalis* or its cultivars.

These sages may be grown in a container.

PROPAGATION

Vegetative cuttings may be taken from terminal growth during the spring and summer. Side shoots along the primary stalks provide an ample supply of cutting material. Cuttings root easily. It is the nature of all of these *Salvia* to spread when the lower branches layer, forming roots. Plants may be obtained by reaching under the sage, and cutting off one of these rooted portions. Cut this branch back to 3 to 6 inches, and pot it up into a container, or plant it out into the garden.

MAINTENANCE

Very EASY! Flowers of *Salvia officinalis* do not need to be deadheaded. Prune lightly at the end of winter to shape the plant and encourage new growth.

Salvia chamaedryoides will produce more flowers for several weeks if the portion that has bloomed is removed. At the end of winter, prune last year's growth back by two-thirds to stimulate new growth for the coming season.

Salvia greggii (autumn sage) is not hardy in my Sierra foothill garden (2700-foot elevation), though it has been successful at elevations of 2500 feet in the foothills, or in a warm microclimate. It survives the occasional ice storm in the Pacific Northwest. It has not been tested for deer-resistance in gardens that I have designed.

Salvia elegans (pineapple sage) is a beautiful fall-blooming perennial that the deer love to eat. It is not winter-hardy at my 2700-foot elevation.

SANTOLINA

Santolina
(santolina)

Santolina is a very tough evergreen (or evergray) shrub, and very attractive in the dry garden. Even those with silver foliage will tolerate a surprising amount of shade. All have similar blooms, an abundance of little round flowerheads. Foliage is strongly aeromatic.

DESCRIPTION

Santolina chamaecyparissus (lavender cotton) is the most commonly seen in gardens. A mature plant is about 2 feet in height in bloom, and as much as 4 feet or more in spread. Size and form will depend on how much it is pruned each year. Flowers are golden. 'Nana' is a dwarf cultivar.

Santolina ericoides **'Lemon Queen'** is more compact, 2 to 2½ feet in spread, than the species, with slightly finer foliage. Flowers are yellow.

Santolina rosmarinifolia (rosemary santolina) is as large as lavender cotton, with gray-green foliage that looks like the foliage of rosemary. It has a wonderful vertical texture when the gray-green stems are supporting fine, tiny, silvery buds. Flowers are golden.

Santolina virens (green santolina) is about the same size as *Santolina* 'Lemon Queen'. It is a rich bright-green in foliage, with yellow flowers.

CULTURAL REQUIREMENTS

Zones 5–9. *Santolina* will grow in the coldest regions of the western, southwestern, and northwestern United States.

Full sun is the best exposure. In partial shade, *Santolina* may be more rangy in its growth habit, and need to be pruned to keep it attractive. All cultivars will tolerate partial shade, including north slopes which receive little sunlight in winter.

Soil should not be rich, but the addition of organic phosphorus and compost is required.

Santolina is a very drought-tolerant plant, and should not be irrigated more than once every 2 to 3 weeks. Drainage must be excellent, especially in winter.

BLOOM

Bloom begins in early summer, and continues for several weeks. The budding stage is very attractive, adding delicate vertical interest in the garden. Flowers are small clusters, forming a ball shape at the end of fine, but strong, upright stems.

Santolina is a good cut flower, and a good everlasting.

It is not necessary to deadhead this evergreen perennial.

SEASONAL INTEREST

The evergreen foliage of santolina is attractive in the garden year-round. Flowers coming into bloom add more interest in late spring, and pleasing color for several weeks in early to midsummer.

The textural interest of the fading flowers is interesting.

Pick a few flowers when they are at the height of their color for winter bouquets.

COMPANION PLANTS AND LANDSCAPE USE

Rosemary is a good companion plant with *Santolina*. Create good contrasts in your garden with varying foliage color and form.

On a large bank, even with hot western exposure, *Santolina* is a good ground cover. It may be allowed to spread without pruning, and its density and height will allow few weeds to germinate.

Santolina is a good plant for the rock garden, or for dry edges.

Iris spuria has lovely contrasting foliage and similar cultural requirements.

Santolina may be used in the dry shade of native oaks, where light is bright.

PROPAGATION

Vegetative cuttings may be taken from *Santolina* for a very long season, from late winter through fall. They root quickly, and should be potted up as soon as new growth shows. As young plants, they are very sensitive to overwatering. Use perlite or fine gravel to ensure good drainage in your potting mix.

MAINTENANCE

If you want a plant with a very rounded or tidy form, pruning right after bloom is important. Use hedge shears, cutting back faded flowers and about a third of the new growth. With this summer pruning, no additional maintenance will be needed at the end of winter.

When no summer pruning is done, removing faded flowers stalks and a light cutting of the foliage at the end of winter is appropriate.

Large plantings on steep banks do not need maintenance. New growth will cover most of the old flower stalks.

Solidago

Solidago
(goldenrod)

In late summer, 2-foot tall goldenrod lined the country dirt road in the rural area of Sonoma County, California, near my family's home. While it was often considered to be the cause of allergies, it was actually the ragweed that was blooming at the same time that was the culprit. It was many years later that I was introduced to a cultivated goldenrod in the Victorian garden of Elizabeth Fitzgerald in Grass Valley, California. Her plants were 5 to 6 feet in height, glorious in bloom. She loved their color and stature, but cursed their spreading habit, so of course she shared a box full of plants for me to add to my own garden.

DESCRIPTION

In my garden, the herbaceous goldenrod given to me by another passionate gardener is 5 to 6 feet in height in bloom, and just keeps spreading. Foliage is dark-green, long, narrow leaves of beautiful form.

Another, *Solidago* 'Golden Baby', is compact and more refined in its growth habit. This plant is 12 to 18 inches in spread, and under 18 inches in height in bloom. Foliage is mid-green. There are other hybrids with heights ranging from 1 to 3 feet.

CULTURAL REQUIREMENTS

Zones 3–10. Herbaceous goldenrod grows in the coldest regions of the western, southwestern, and northwestern United States.

Appropriate exposures include sun, to light shade where summers are hot.

Goldenrod thrives in good garden soil with the addition of organic compost and phosphorus. As a wildflower, it often grows in very poor soils, but the hybrid cultivars definitely need more fertile soil. Soil does not need to be rich. Mulch to conserve moisture.

The taller goldenrod in my garden is fairly drought-tolerant, but receives irrigation water every 2 weeks in the heat of the summer, especially when temperatures are above 85°F. Smaller hybrid cultivars seem to need irrigation once a week in summer heat, even when they are mulched.

BLOOM

The goldenrod all have a characteristic arching plume of yellow flowers, opening in late summer. The larger the plant, the larger the plume and blooming stalk. Flowering plumes are a very attractive addition to the late summer border, lasting for several weeks.

All are excellent cut flowers. To dry these flowers for everlastings, cut the stalks when they are at the height of color, and lay them on a table in shade. Hanging them upside down to dry will alter their beautiful arching shape.

Flowers are not deadheaded in my garden because the plumes turn to golden-brown fluffy seedheads.

SEASONAL INTEREST

The taller goldenrod is a strong foliage plant from early spring until it comes into bloom in late summer. This is a long season of interest from the attractive foliage.

Smaller cultivars are equally attractive, but not as bold.

With bloom from late summer into fall, and the attractive seedheads following bloom, goldenrod extends its season of interest until winter's chill ends the display.

COMPANION PLANTS AND LANDSCAPE USE

The taller *Solidago* may outdistance most perennials and even some shrubs in height, but perennial sunflower (*Helianthus maximilianii*) is similar in height, aggressiveness of spread, and beauty of both foliage and flowers. Use them near one another, but allow each room to spread.

Smaller goldenrods have many uses in the border, especially with the late-blooming blue flowers of bluebeard (*Caryopteris incana*) and plumbago (*Ceratostigma plumbaginoides* and *C. willmottianum*).

The smallest goldenrods are good in an irrigated rock garden, or in a container.

The yellow flowers of goldenrod are very attractive with the ornamental grasses as they turn to golden-brown in the fall. Match the size of the grass to that of the goldenrod. The late blooms or dark seedheads of black-eyed Susan (*Rudbeckia fulgida* 'Goldsturm') are a perfect addition to this fall display.

PROPAGATION

Those goldenrods that spread aggressively may be divided in late fall or winter after cutting them back, or in early spring when growth first shows. There is plenty of material for dividing, with a plant that has been in the ground for just a year.

Vegetative cuttings may be taken from smaller cultivars in spring or early summer, before stalks elongate for bloom.

MAINTENANCE

Deadheading is not necessary right after bloom because the seed stage is attractive. Cut flowering stalks back when they are no longer attractive from your perspective.

Winter maintenance consists of cutting all foliage and stalks back to the crown. Renew the mulch with new compost.

TANACETUM

Tanacetum parthenium
(feverfew)

Tanacetum parthenium 'Aureum'

Feverfew is a coveted perennial in my garden, its lacy evergreen foliage a pleasing texture in sun and shade, and its white flowers a welcome addition in almost every nook and cranny. This drought-tolerant perennial self-sows readily, but its ease of culture should not detract from its value in the landscape. This perennial was previously classified as a *Chrysanthemum parthenium*.

DESCRIPTION

Tanacetum parthenium is a strong perennial with delicate, lacy, evergreen foliage that is aeromatic. Height and spread depend on soil fertility. Soil that is slightly improved will usually produce a plant that is 2 to 3 feet in height and spread in bloom. Multiple white flowers are produced on branching stalks. Foliage is bright to dark-green.

The cultivar 'Aureum' has gold-green foliage with smaller sprays of the typical white flowers. It is also smaller in growth habit, to 2 feet in height and spread.

Out of bloom, both the species and its cultivars are evergreen mounds of lacy foliage.

CULTURAL REQUIREMENTS

Zones 3–9. *Tanacetum parthenium* will grow in the coldest regions of the western, southwestern, and northwestern United States.

The best exposure for the green-leafed feverfew is full sun to light shade. 'Aureum' will grow well in partial to deep shade, and needs some afternoon shade in hot-summer areas.

Do not overfertilize the soil. It will cause the plant to grow larger and more rangy. Soil that is not rich, but is improved with some organic compost and phosphorus, will produce a plant that is compact and does not need staking.

Mulches will conserve moisture. A mulched plant is very drought-tolerant. While *Tanacetum parthenium* will tolerate irrigation once a week, it does not need it. Irrigation once every 2 to 3 weeks is adequate. In a wet spring, no irrigation is needed for the first wave of bloom.

A rugged perennial that will adapt to full sun or shade, fertile or lean soils, a broad range of temperatures and moisture availability, feverfew is a forgiving perennial. It even does well where there is root competition from nearby plants.

BLOOM

Small, white flowerheads less than an inch in diameter open on multiple strong, but fine, branching stalks. Attractive flowers vary in form, from rounded balls to open daisies with the centers visible.

The blooming lasts for a few weeks, beginning in late spring or early summer. This white is a highlight of my garden when the feverfew is in bloom.

Feverfew is an excellent cut flower for large and small arrangements.

When bloom fades, deadhead by removing stalks to the crown, or to new shoots at the base of the stalk. If this is done right after flowers fade, and feverfew receives some irrigation water during the heat of the summer, there will be a repeat bloom. The height of the plant may be under 2 feet for the second wave of bloom in late summer.

Tanacetum parthenium grown as a wildflower, with no summer irrigation, will most likely bloom only in the spring.

If you are seed-saving, you may leave a few flowerheads on the plant, allowing the seed to mature. Where the season is short, this may have to be done with the first wave of bloom. In my garden, where Indian summer lingers, seeds are saved from the second wave of bloom. They are scattered where more plants are desired.

SEASONAL INTEREST

The lacy evergreen foliage of *Tanacetum parthenium* is desirable year-round. In bloom, it is a beautiful perennial, complementing other colors with its strong white.

The gold foliage of *Tanacetum parthenium* 'Aureum' glows in the subdued light of the shade garden.

COMPANION PLANTS AND LANDSCAPE USE

Feverfew is an attractive edger, although it will be taller with the first bloom.

Tanacetum parthenium is an excellent addition to the drought-tolerant garden in full sun. The white flowers will complement the gold flowers of *Achillea filipendulina* or *Santolina*, the blue of sage (*Salvia*), and all the lavenders.

The cultivar 'Aureum' is perfect for the dry shade garden, combined with ladybells (*Adenophora confusa*) or *Euphorbia amygdaloides robbiae*.

Because they will tolerate irrigation, all the feverfews play an important role in the herbaceous border of a large garden, or as a single plant in a small garden. As a container plant, they must be in a large container (at least 5 gallons) to maximize their beauty. Stressed plants are not attractive.

PROPAGATION

Allow plants to self-sow in moderation. In mild climates, lift plants in fall and place them in their permanent location. In colder climates, wait until late winter or very early spring.

Seed may be saved, flowerheads broken apart, and seed scattered on the compost mulch of a planting bed in fall. Do not cover the seed.

Vegetative cuttings may also be made from side shoots in late spring or in summer.

MAINTENANCE

Deadhead feverfew right after the first bloom to stimulate the second bloom in late summer. Cut back faded flower stalks to the crown or to 3 inches, to encourage new basal leaves to form.

TEUCRIUM

Teucrium x *lucidrys, T. chamaedrys*
(germander)

Teucrium x *lucidrys* is one of the smallest of the evergreen subshrubs in my garden, a plant that has use as an edging, or mixed with herbaceous or evergreen perennials. Germanders are tough plants, growing well even in rocky soil where other plants struggle.

Teucrium x *lucidrys*

DESCRIPTION

Teucrium x *lucidrys* is an evergreen with small, glossy dark-green leaves and attractive rose-purple flowers. Branching stalks are upright on a slightly sprawling plant. Height is 15 to 18 inches in bloom, 12 to 15 inches out of bloom. Each plant spreads to about 2 to 3 feet, but is easily pruned if a more compact plant is desired.

CULTURAL REQUIREMENTS

Zones 5–10. *Teucrium* x *lucidrys* does well in the coldest regions of the western, southwestern, and northwestern United States. It is one of the few evergreen subshrubs that will survive temperatures below 5°F.

This green-leafed germander will grow in full hot sun or light shade.

The best plant form is in full sun. Plants grown in shade will be more likely to sprawl.

While it will grow in rocky soil, and in soil of low fertility, germander is stronger when a small amount of compost has been added. The addition of organic phosphorus, will strengthen the root growth and the flowering.

Mulch may be of organic materials, or small rocks, or gravel.

Teucrium x *lucidrys* is drought-tolerant, but will tolerate irrigation every 2 to 3 weeks. If soil drainage is excellent, irrigation may be more frequent with no damage to the plant. The lower leaves on an overwatered plant will turn yellow.

BLOOM

Flowers of *Teucrium* x *lucidrys* are rosy-purple, clustered in spikes on the upright stalks. Bloom begins in mid to late summer, and lasts for many weeks, even without deadheading.

Fading flowers are still attractive, with a light-pink hue that fades to brown in the seed stage. In the seed stage, the stalks continue to add a nice texture.

SEASONAL INTEREST

Germander is an evergreen plant with year-round interest. In winter its glossy leaves appear as fresh as they do in the spring. A late-bloomer, this wonderful perennial adds color when many other garden treasures are fading.

COMPANION PLANTS AND LANDSCAPE USE

Its low-growing habit allows germander to be used as an edging, which becomes a focal point in an herbaceous border in the winter.

Use *Teucrium* x *lucidrys* in the rock garden, or in a small garden. Because it is a compact evergreen, germander becomes a structural plant in the smaller landscape.

All of the lavenders and lavandins *(Lavandula)*, and sages *(Salvia)* are good companion plants.

One of my favorite combinations is *Teucrium* x *lucidrys* with the low-growing threadleaf tickseed *(Coreopsis verticillata* 'Moonbeam'). Another great companion plant is *Penstemon pinifolius*.

Like a miniature boxwood, this germander may be pruned to be a small "hedge" along a walkway or in a formal herb garden.

Germander is good in a container.

Bulbs should be planted 3 feet away from the center of a germander.

PROPAGATION

Vegetative cuttings may be taken even when the plant is in bloom, from side shoots which offer a continual supply of cutting material.

Branching stems may also layer, forming roots. These may be "divided" by removing the stem from the parent plant, cutting the separated piece back to 3 inches, and potting it up into a container. This is best done in fall.

MAINTENANCE

Teucrium x *lucidrys* does not need to be deadheaded, unless you prefer a more tidy plant.

When flowering stalks are removed in fall or winter, use hedge or grass clippers to cut back the portion that has bloomed, and also remove a portion (about one-third to one-half)) of the nonblooming branches. This pruning will stimulate new growth in the spring.

Teucrium x *lucidrys* 'Prostratum' is a very attractive evergreen germander, under 6 inches in height in bloom. Cultural requirements are the same as for *Teucrium* x *lucidrys*. This is an excellent rock garden specimen, or very low edging plant.

Teucrium cossonii majoricum (T. cussonii, T. majoricum) is a gray-leafed germander which must be grown in full sun with excellent drainage, especially in the winter. Its mauve flowers are in clusters on low stems, opening midsummer and continuing through fall. If your plant slows in bloom, shear off faded flowers. This is a gem!

Verbena bonariensis

VERBENA

Verbena
(verbena, vervain)

Hardy verbenas are herbaceous perennials needing heat to thrive.

DESCRIPTION

Verbena bonariensis is very tall, up to 5 feet in height. Strong stalks, nearly leafless, support clusters of red-purple flowers, with an airy appearance. Branching stems from the primary stalk have smaller flowerheads, equally colorful. The color of each cluster lasts for several weeks. Each plant is about a foot in width. Low dark-green leaves are most noticeable before the plant begins bloom.

   Verbena rigida (*V. venosa*) is 1 to 2 feet tall, with deep-purple flowers.

Plants spread aggressively by stolons. Dark-green leaves are attractive prior to and during bloom.

CULTURAL REQUIREMENTS

Zones 7–10. *Verbena bonariensis* will grow in the foothills of the Sierra Nevada where winter temperatures are above 10°F. *Verbena rigida* will grow in the coldest regions of the western, southwestern, and north-western United States.

Verbena are rugged perennials that thrive in hot, arid climates. Full sun is the best exposure.

Soil should not be rich. In fact, vervain does well in poor, rocky soils. However, the addition of organic phosphorus is always important. The addition of compost should be for slight enrichment of the existing soil, for moisture retention, and for good winter drainage.

Verbena is drought-tolerant. It may be watered every 2 to 3 weeks, or less frequently. Over-irrigation may weaken this perennial.

BLOOM

See description. *Verbena bonariensis* is rosy-purple on tall stalks. *Verbena rigida* is a rich, deep-purple. Flowerheads of both species are very long-lasting. They both bloom for months, from early summer into fall.

Both are excellent cut flowers. Butterflies love this perennial.

Because the flowerheads are so long-lasting, there is little need to deadhead during the summer. When flowers do fade, cut to the next leaf axil. The stalks may continue to branch and bloom.

COMPANION PLANTS AND LANDSCAPE USE

Both vervains are excellent in the dry garden. Most other plants in this garden will have a shorter bloom.

A large stand of either species is a focal point. *Verbena bonariensis*, especially, has more impact in the landscape when several plants are grouped together. Its effect is still airy, but very colorful.

Sundrops (*Oenothera tetragona*), with its bright yellow flowers, is a beautiful complement to the purple of *Verbena rigida*. As sundrops stops blooming, the verbena continues into fall. This vervain is also very lovely with Santa Barbara daisy (*Erigeron karvinskianus*), *Lavandula*, and the sages (*Salvia*).

PROPAGATION

Verbena bonariensis self-sows easily. Young plants may be moved to their permanent location in fall. Or save seed and scatter it on compost where you want the plants to grow.

Verbena rigida spreads by stolons. Mature plants may be divided in fall, or new plants may be lifted when they first show in spring. Make sure that the fleshy stolon has small feeder roots.

MAINTENANCE

Very EASY! Deadhead as needed. Cut back all stalks to the crown with winter cleanup.

Verbena Tapien hybrids are not deer-resistant, and they are not hardy in most gardens where the elevation is over 2500 feet.

ZAUSCHNERIA

Zauschneria
(California fuchsia)

Zauschneria californica (Epilobium californica) is a California native undaunted by hot, dry summers. It doesn't even begin to bloom until many other perennials have finished their show. This semi-evergreen perennial is not a fuchsia, though its common name would suggest this.

DESCRIPTION

California fuchsia has varying cultivars. The most dependable, hardy one in my garden has been *Zauschneria californica*. With beautiful silvery-gray leaves to 1½ inches, it spreads easily to establish stands with scarlet flowers in late summer.

CULTURAL REQUIREMENTS

Zones 8–10 are often recommended, but California fuchsia will grow in fairly cold regions of the western United States, such as Denver,

Colorado. In the coldest areas, it is herbaceous and may need to be mulched in winter.

Zauschneria californica is definitely a good performer for hot, dry climates. This is a full-sun plant.

Soil should not be rich, but the addition of organic phosphorus is important. Small amounts of compost may be added to improve soil.

A native in dry summer climates, this tough perennial is drought-tolerant. Do not overwater. If drainage is good, California fuchsia may tolerate irrigation every three weeks, but it does not need any water in summer once it has established.

BLOOM

Zauschneria californica (Epilobium californica)

Bright-scarlet, trumpet-shaped flowers, up to 2 inches in length, are a call to hummingbirds. Flowers begin opening in late summer, and continue for several weeks with each leafy stalk supporting several flowers. The combination of scarlet and silver is quite striking.

Flowers may be used for cut arrangements, but do not last long.

Deadheading is not necessary, but may allow more flowers to open, since the plant will not be putting its energy into the seed production.

SEASONAL INTEREST

In areas of mild fall or winter temperatures, the foliage of *Zauschneria californica* may continue to be an attractive, silver-gray addition to the dry garden. In colder regions, snows may flatten the stalks.

The flowering season lasts for several weeks from late summer into fall.

COMPANION PLANTS AND LANDSCAPE USE

Companion plants must also thrive in full sun and low irrigation. There are many perennials and subshrubs that will, including *Lavandula, Salvia, Achillea, Artemisia, Romneya,* and *Verbena.* California fuchsia adds an exciting new color to the dry garden.

Compatible ornamental grasses include *Stipa, Festuca,* and *Bouteloua gracilis.*

PROPAGATION

The roots of California fuchsia are easily divided during the dormant season. Division is best in late fall after cutting the stalks back to the crown.

California fuchsia may be propagated by cuttings taken in spring, but they are very sensitive to overwatering.

MAINTENANCE

Very EASY! Deadheading may increase the flowering, but is not necessary. Abundant bloom will occur without it. When plants begin to look shabby in winter, cut all the stalks back to the crown.

APPENDIX 1

DEER-RESISTANT EDGING PERENNIALS

The deer have not been aggressive about eating most of the low-growing perennials in my garden, although they do have their favorites: *Iberis sempervirens*, *Dianthus plumarius*, and the wonderful dwarf *Aster novi-belgii* cultivars. Included here is a list of the edging plants and other low-growing perennials that have been grown without deer damage in my garden. Details for some of these plants are in this book. Others will be in volume 2 of the "yucky flower" series: rock garden & edging perennials!

Achillea Clavennae

Achillea tomentosa 'Maynard's Gold'

Achillea tomentosa 'Moonlight'

Aegopodium podagraria 'Variegatum'

Ajuga reptans

Alchemilla mollis

Alyssum montanum 'Mountain Gold'

Alyssum petraeus

Alyssum tortuosum

Arabis albida 'Variegata'

Arabis alpina (*A. caucasica*)

Arabis Fernando-Coburgi

Arabis procurrens

Arctostaphylos uva-ursi

Armeria maritima

Artemisia schmidtiana 'Silver Mound'

Artemisia versicolor (*A. canescens*)

Aubrieta deltoidea

Aubrieta gracilis

Aurinia saxatilis

Campanula poscharskyana

Cerastium Bierbersteinii

Cerastium tomentosum

Ceratostigma plumbaginoides

Chamaemelum nobile 'Flore Pleno'

Coreopsis verticillata 'Moonbeam'

Cotoneaster 'Tom Thumb'

Cymbalaria muralis

Delosperma nubigenum

Dianthus 'Tiny Rubies'

Dianthus freynii

Dianthus gratianopolitanus

Dianthus microlepis

Dianthus petraeus ssp. *noeanus*

Dianthus simulans

Dianthus squarrosus

Dicentra eximia

Digitalis lutea

Erigeron karvinskianus

Erinus alpinus

Erysimum helvaticum (formerly E. Kotschyanum)

Gaillardia 'Goblin'

Galium odoratum

Geranium sanguineum 'Cedric Morris'

Geranium x cantabrigiense

Geranium x cantabrigiense

Gypsophila cerastioides

Gypsophila repens

Herniaria glabra

Lavandula angustifolia 'Vera'

Leucanthem x superbum 'Snow Lady'

Lychnis Flos-Jovis

Lysimachia nummularia (the deer eat taller species of Lysimachia)

Myosotis scorpioides

Nepeta 'Six Hills Giant'

Nepeta x faassenii

Origanum laevigatum

Origanum pulchellum

Origanum vulgare 'Aureum'

Origanum vulgare nanum

Penstemon fruticosus 'Purple Haze'

Penstemon gentianoides

Penstemon hirsutus

Penstemon pinifolius

Phlox subulata

Potentilla canadensis

Rosmarinus 'Lockwood de Forest'

Rubus calycinoides

Saponaria pumilio

Scleranthus uniflorus

Sedum album 'Athoum'

Sedum album 'Faro Form'

Sedum album subspecies

Silene alpestris

Silene vulgaris ssp. maritima

Solidago 'Golden Baby'

Stachys byzantina

Teucrium chamaedrys 'Compacta'

Teucrium cussonii Majoricum

Teucrium polinium

Thymus 'Doone's Valley'

Thymus citriodorus

Thymus glabrescens

Thymus herba-barona

Thymus nitens

Thymus praecox arcticus

Thymus pseudolanuginosus

Thymus pulegioides

Thymus serpyllum

Thymus vulgaris

Verbena rigida (V. venosa)

Veronica Allionii

Veronica liwanensis

Veronica peduncularis 'Georgia Blue'

Veronica 'Waterperry'

Viola labradorica

Zauschneria (Epilobium) latifolia

APPENDIX 2

OTHER PERENNIALS THAT MAY BE DEER-RESISTANT

Plants that have not been eaten in my garden but that have not been tested in other deer areas:

Bergenia	Melissa officinalis
Diascia	Potentilla fruticosa
Epimedium	Salvia pitcheri
Eupatorium	Senecio
Kniphofia	Verbascum
Liriope	

A list of plants that have sometimes been deer-resistant (a few flowers nibbled, browsing one year, but not another) :

Acanthus	Hemerocallis
Anchusa	Mimulus
Asarum	Myosotis
Bergenia	Origanum laevigatum
Boltonia	Platycodon
Convallaria	Sidalcea
Epimedium	Viola odorata
Heliopsis	

APPENDIX 3

PLANTS THAT ARE NOT DEER-RESISTANT, BUT ARE ON "DEER-RESISTANT" PLANT LISTS

How do plants continue to be placed on "deer-resistant" and "definitely deer-resistant" plant lists?!? The deer love *Agapanthus* and *Aquilegia!* And others…

Carolyn's list of perennials & some subshrubs listed on several lists as "deer-resistant", which are definitely eaten by deer in her garden, and in other western gardens!!!

Achillea millefolium hybrids

Agapanthus

Alstroemeria

Anemone

Aquilegia

Armeria Formosa hybrids

Aruncus

Ascelpias

Aster

Astilbe

Campanula
(*C. poscharskyana* is deer-resistant)

Canna

Centranthus ruber

Ceratostigma griffithii

Chrysanthemum

Cistus spp.

Corydalis

Delphinium

Dianthus plumarius

Diascia

Euphorbia amygdaloides rubra, E. griffithii

Filipendula

Geranium (see text for species not eaten)

Geum

Helianthemum

Helianthus multiflorus

Hemerocallis

Hibiscus

Hosta

Iberis

Limonium

Lupinus

Lychnis chalcedonica

Lysimachia punctata,
L. clethroides

Monarda didyma

Oenothera speciosa

Penstemon gloxinoides
(see text for species not eaten)

Phlox paniculata

Physalis alkekengi

Physostegia virginiana

Primula

Rudbeckia triloba

Salvia greggii, S. elegans

Saponaria ocymoides

Scabiosa

Sedum
(except a few compact
rock garden species)

Sisyrinchium californicum

Stokesia

Symphytum officinale (comfrey)

Thalictrum

Tulbaghia violacea (society garlic)

Veronica longifolia
(low-growing species, used as
groundcovers or edgers, are not
eaten by deer)

Viola odorata
(*Viola labradorica* is usually
left alone)

INDEX

ORDER FORM

Telephone orders: Call (530) 272-4362.

Email orders: orders@gardenwisdompress.com

Postal orders: Garden Wisdom Press, P.O. Box 992, Grass Valley CA 95945

DEER IN MY GARDEN!

THE YUCKY PLANT SERIES

VOL. 1: PERENNIALS & SUBSHRUBS

Please send _____ copies @ $19.95.

NAME _____

ADDRESS _____

CITY _____ STATE _____ ZIP _____

TELEPHONE _____

EMAIL ADDRESS _____

Sales tax: Please add 7.375% for books shipped to California addresses.

Shipping by air:

U.S.: $4.00 for first book and $2.00 for each additional book.

International: $9.00 for first book; $5.00 for each additional book.

If the shipping costs exceed these amounts, the purchaser will be notified prior to shipment.

Payment by check or money order should accompany this form.

For payment thru PayPal, order online at **www.gardenwisdompress.com**

ORDER FORM

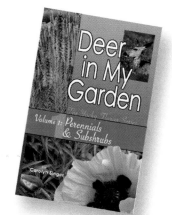

Telephone orders: Call (530) 272-4362.

Email orders: orders@gardenwisdompress.com

Postal orders: Garden Wisdom Press, P.O. Box 992, Grass Valley CA 95945

DEER IN MY GARDEN!

THE YUCKY PLANT SERIES

VOL. 1: PERENNIALS & SUBSHRUBS

Please send _____ copies @ $19.95.

NAME_____

ADDRESS _____

CITY _____ STATE _____ ZIP _____

TELEPHONE _____

EMAIL ADDRESS _____

Sales tax: Please add 7.375% for books shipped to California addresses.

Shipping by air:
U.S.: $4.00 for first book and $2.00 for each additional book.
International: $9.00 for first book; $5.00 for each additional book.
If the shipping costs exceed these amounts, the purchaser will be notified prior to shipment.

Payment by check or money order should accompany this form.

For payment thru PayPal, order online at **www.gardenwisdompress.com**